# Hazel Grove
# to Armageddon

### An appreciative commemoration
### of the men of Hazel Grove, Cheshire
### who died as a consequence of
### World War 1.

## Sponsored by Frederic Robinson Ltd
## & The Royal Bank of Scotland

Published by
Stockport M.B.C. Community Services Division
and Stockport Libraries

Copyright c. 1998
John D. Eaton.
5, Redcar Close, Hazel Grove,
Stockport, SK7 4SQ

The illustration on the <u>Front Cover</u> has been taken from : The Manchester
Guardian History of the War, Vol. IX, 1919-1920, (1920), p44 (top
illustration). The illustration on the <u>Back Cover</u> has been taken from
Vol. V p144 (bottom illustration).

ISBN 0 905164 80 6

Printed and bound in England by
Tom Dolan, Reprographics Manager, Reprographics Department,
Town Hall, Stockport,
SK1 3RS

# Acknowledgements

This book could not have been written without the help of the following. I am deeply grateful to all of them :-

Mrs. J Bratherton; Mrs. D Clough; Rev. M Collins; Mrs. M Cook; C Curling; K J Daniels; J Downs; R Hadfield; E Holebrook; K Holebrook; B Kilday; T McNicol; J Parker; B Redmond; J Skeen; Mrs. A Tate; S Tomlinson; Mrs. E Warren and P.Wood.

The staffs of Stockport Local Heritage Library; Manchester Central Library; Cheshire Record Office; Greater Manchester Record Office; Stalybridge Library; Commonwealth War Graves Commission; Imperial War Museum; Australian Archives; National Archives of Canada; Coldstream Guards; Middlesex Regt. Association and the staffs of the following museums - Cheshire Regt.; King's Regt.; King's Own Royal Lancashire Regt.; Lancashire Fusiliers; City of Lancaster; Manchester Regt.; National Museum & Galleries on Merseyside; Northumberland Fusiliers; Queen's Own Highlanders; RAMC; Royal Air Force; Royal Greenjackets; Royal Regt. of Wales; Sherwood Foresters; Shropshire Regt.; Staffordshire Regt. and Welch Regt..

David Reid of Stockport Local Heritage Library for his help in publishing this book.

Messrs. Frederic Robinson Ltd. and The Royal Bank of Scotland for their sponsorship, without which this book could not have been published.

Finally, to my friend Michael Race and my wife Patricia. Without the enormous effort, help and advice given by both of them, this book would not have been possible. Many thanks.

~~~~~

# CONTENTS

~~~~

# HISTORICAL INTRODUCTION

"To those gallant men of Hazel Grove who gave all they had to give ....." were the opening words of the speech given by Ernest Bagshawe JP, of Poise House, Hazel Grove, who as the President of the War Memorial Committee unveiled the village Memorial at 3 p.m. on Sunday 11 November 1923. He knew what they had given. His son Geoffrey's name was on the Memorial. The Deputy President of the Committee was Alfred Hallam JP who for a considerable period during the war had been the Chairman of Hazel Grove and Bramhall Urban District Council, and he too knew. His son Frank had his name on the Memorial.

Mrs. Sarah Clough of 3 Daniel Street also knew. Her two sons were on the Memorial. She was a widow, living in probably some of the worst housing in the village. In addition, her daughter's husband had been a prisoner of war. She had no sons left.

Naturally, more residents of London Road were killed than any other road, simply because more people lived on it than any other road, but Grundey Street was particularly badly hit. Residents of numbers 6,8, and 10 were killed.

Altogether there were nine sets of brothers among the 111 names originally entered on the Memorial. The Holebrook family fared worst - two brothers and two of their nephews died. The most poignant was perhaps the plight of the Jones brothers who died on consecutive days, even though they served in different regiments on different parts of the Western Front.

The shortest length of service was that of Albert Butterworth who at the age of 18 had been in the Army for five weeks, whilst the youngest was Henry Pillatt, who contracted an illness 'whilst serving his country' as a Boy Scout. He was 16. Thirteen men survived the war only to succumb later, including the most decorated man on the Memorial, Stephen Vickers, who was awarded the Military Cross and the Distinguished Flying Cross. He survived the rigours of the trenches before transferring to the Royal Flying Corps where he completed 75 successful bombing missions. Fate dealt him a poor reward, however, because in February 1919 he died of pneumonia.

At least two other men, who had definite connections with the village, have never had their names inscribed upon the Memorial and details of them have also been included in this book.

The effects of the war continued to be felt by those who returned, many suffering nightmares and pain for the rest of their lives. Three names were entered after the Memorial was erected, the last dying in August 1943. By this time, there were already a considerable number of names for inclusion for World War 2.

When World War 1 started on 4 August 1914, Hazel Grove had a population of about 7000 people. It was not a wealthy village. The vast majority of its inhabitants were "working class" people employed in the local mills and factories or even in the coal mines in nearby villages. Norbury School Log Book contains regular comments complaining of poor attendance due to measles, chickenpox, poor weather and even children being kept away from school to help with the potato harvest.

The comments of the School Inspectors show a school which was to some extent overcrowded, with its fabric beginning to show signs of age, battling against parental indifference. Ringworm was found on the foreheads of pupils on a number of occasions and there are regular comments in the Log Book about new children turning up at the school at the age of seven or eight who had not previously attended school anywhere and did not know their alphabet. With a few exceptions, the school felt it had succeeded if it turned out pupils who knew their Bible and had a grasp of the "three Rs".

Few people had travelled far outside the village, though being within easy reach of Manchester and Buxton because of the railway line, it was not as isolated as many communities at that time. The War changed all that.

The young men of the village flocked to the Colours as they did in every other part of the country, all hoping to get involved in a little bit of the action before the war ended, which was confidently predicted to be before Christmas by the people who knew about these things. There was a chance to travel abroad, something until then beyond their wildest dreams, and to have some fun and adventure. Tragically it all went wrong for so many of them.

Apart from the excitement of the first recruits joining up and going away, and the influx of a number of Belgian refugees into the village, at first, the war had little effect on Hazel Grove life. Harold Brooks of Commercial Road was reported as having been killed in action at Mons on 26 August 1914. He was a regular soldier who had enlisted into the King's Royal Lancaster Regiment six years before. It was however a false alarm - he had in fact been taken prisoner and spent the rest of the war in a Prisoner of War Camp.

The first real casualty came on 13 October 1914 when William Bartlett was killed but it was May 1915 before the next, when the slow trickle of deaths which later became a flood, began to be reported. Even so, the village seemed to be getting off quite lightly at first. On the first day of the Battle of the Somme, 1 July 1916, when British casualties were nearly 60,000 in one day, only one man from Hazel Grove was killed, though as the battle progressed over the following five months, to finally peter out due to exhaustion in the mud, rain and cold of late November 1916, fifteen had been killed.

1917 brought, amongst other horrors, the Third Battle of Ypres (commonly known as the Battle of Passchendaele). More than any other battle, the mud and desolation of this time epitomises the First World War. 15 men from Hazel Grove were to die during the three and a half months it lasted.

The worst year was 1918. Desperate to finish the war before the American Army could get into the field and before the British could bring their new weapon, the Tank, fully into play, the Germans made a massive effort to break the British Army. The village had a part to play in this new weapon. The company Mirrlees, Bickerton & Day Ltd, which had set up the world's first purpose-built factory to manufacture diesel engines on Bramhall Moor Lane in 1908, provided not only a number of servicemen from amongst its employees, but it also built the diesel engines which drove a large proportion of the tanks. In addition, it tested some tanks on what later became the 2nd fairway of its golf course.

At 0440 hours on the morning of 21 March 1918 and in thick mist, forty three enemy divisions burst upon the 42 mile-long, weakly held, Fifth Army front on the Somme. Prior to the attack, the defenders had undergone a shattering bombardment by nearly 6000 guns during which smoke and gas shells were mixed liberally with high explosives. Fog and smoke blotted out aerial observation and blinded our troops. Units were surrounded and in many cases annihilated almost before they realised what was happening.

Companies, battalions and even divisions were decimated and some virtually ceased to exist. Communications broke down and a serious lack of reserves meant that little could be done at first. However, by 26 March the Germans were exhausted, but they renewed their offensive on 9 April, driving a further wedge into the British line. All the gains of the battle of the Somme were lost before reserves could be brought in, first to stem the tide and then to provide the capacity to strike back. In a period of six weeks the losses were staggering- nearly 240,000 British and over 348,000 German casualties.(Flanders Then and Now by John Giles). Further attacks by the Germans in the Ypres area resulted in the loss of all the gains of the Third Battle of Ypres.

On 8 August 1918 the British counter-attacked, sweeping an increasingly demoralised German Army before them. Even so, the enemy continued to fight tenaciously, inflicting heavy casualties on the Allied troops before the War was ended by the Armistice at 11 a.m. on the morning of Monday 11 November 1918.

For Hazel Grove 1918 had taken the lives of 45 of its young men, and the village, like most of the rest of the world, was never to be the same again.

Britain and its Empire lost approximately one million men out of the nine million who served. France and Germany fared even worse, but the lessons were not learned and, in 1945 the process of collecting names to enter on the Memorial began again.

The idea of a War Memorial was first put forward before the war had ended but people's minds were not fully tuned to the idea until after the victory celebrations had begun to die down. Hazel Grove had a double reason to celebrate because on 6 December 1918 the Stockport Advertiser was able to announce that one of the village's sons - Private Wilfred Wood of 52 Chester Road, had been awarded the Victoria Cross for his bravery in Italy on 28 October 1918. For the parents of William Swindells however there was no joy. He was a member of the same battalion as Wilfred Wood ( 10 Bn. Northumberland Fusiliers) but he died on that same 28 October.

The various churches quickly set out to commemorate their members who had died, but despite a letter to the Stockport Advertiser on 3 January 1919 suggesting a memorial for all the Hazel Grove fallen, it took some time to decide how to proceed. Eventually, on 16 December 1920 a meeting was held in the Mechanics Institute (now the Civic Hall) and a committee was formed.

On 4 January 1921 the site was agreed upon and this was later confirmed when Peter Pearce, who owned land next to the proposed site, gave some of it to the village on the condition that it was used to increase the area of the Memorial.

The cost of erecting the Memorial and landscaping the area was to be met by public subscription, and numerous activities, including sports, a music festival and processions took place in an effort to raise funds. The "Land fit for Heroes " promised by David Lloyd George at the end of the War did not, however, materialise, and the recession meant that the many unemployed people in the village could contribute little, if anything, to the fund . Various local worthies and companies made donations, including Ernest Bagshawe, who gave £100, and Hollins Mill (which Bagshawe owned and at which several of the fallen had worked) gave £150.

Despite this, several appeals to the local populace had to be made before the total cost of about £2000 was achieved. It was stated that the Memorial was " not to be the gift of a few, but of everyone in the village."

The Cross itself is 20 feet high and the contractor to build it was Mr. J.W.Hulme whose firm is of course still the village monumental mason. In an effort to help the unemployed, many of whom were returned servicemen, wherever possible all the labour was supplied by local men. In fact, 75% of the money subscribed was spent on wages in the village and of the remaining 25%, only a small proportion was spent on materials which had to be obtained from elsewhere.

Finally the day of the unveiling arrived. The proceedings began with a procession from the Council School in Chapel Street. The school had been opened in 1912 so is unlikely to have supplied any of the names on the Memorial, but the village was proud to have such a school and the Memorial Committee decreed that this would be a fit starting point for the procession. Consisting of the Committee members, Councillors, Clergy, Overseers and Guardians, a detachment of the Stockport Medium Battery of the Royal Garrison Artillery, local ex-servicemen, The Hazel Grove Silver Band, St. John's Ambulance Brigade, Boy Scouts, Cubs, Girl Guides and Police, the procession wound its way via Chapel Street, Hazel Street, Commercial Road and London Road to the site.

Relatives of the deceased were allowed into the gardens by ticket and the general public were to be allowed in after the ceremony. The procession arrived at 3p.m. and the gates were ceremonially opened by Ernest Bagshawe with a key handed to him by Peter Pearce. The service was conducted by Rev.A.J.Humphreys, the Vicar of Norbury, the local parish church, and large crowds witnessed both the procession and the opening.

After the speech by Mr. Bagshawe, the Last Post and Reveille were sounded by buglers of the Artillery and the National Anthem was sung.The 111 names were then read out and relatives placed wreaths at the base of the Memorial.

The gardens now form a small oasis of greenery in the centre of the village and are passed, unseen, by literally thousands of people every day as they hurry by in their vehicles on the A6. The journeys they carry out are by courtesy of the men whose names are inscribed at the base of the cross which stands sentinel over them. With the inclusion of later deaths, the total on the Memorial reached 114.

By looking at the appropriate Regimental Histories and War Diaries, it is possible to find out where and how their battalion was occupied on the date of their death and so get an idea of the circumstances under which they died. For one or two, precise details of how they died have remained, but regrettably where a serviceman was in a very large regiment such as The Machine Gun Corps or The Royal Artillery, there were so many small independent units that it is very difficult to trace the exact details. To put it in context, The Royal Artillery was larger than the Royal Navy and the Royal Navy was the largest Navy in the world.

"We will remember them," says the inscription on the Memorial. This book is an attempt to help to do just that. Some have left little to be traced and, as a result, very little can now be told about their lives. Others have left considerably more, and we can see what they looked like and know what people thought about them. There are also one or two mysteries which, so far, remain unsolved.

Let us not forget.

~~~~

# CHRONOLOGICAL LIST OF DEATHS

13/10/1914   William George Bartlett ( 1 Bn Cheshire Regt.)

8/5/1915     John Grady ( 2 Bn Kings Own Royal Lancaster Regt.)
13/5/1915   Geoffrey Hamilton Bagshawe ( 1 Bn Royal Dragoon Guards)
16/5/1915   Gilbert William Stanton (1 Bn Royal Welch Fusiliers)
25/6/1915   Frederick Bailey (1 Bn Cheshire Regt.)
20/7/1915   Emrys Thomas ( 7 Bn Manchester Regt.)
3/10/1915   Joseph Burgess ( 2 Bn Cheshire Regt.)

13/2/1916   Samuel Condliffe ( 19 Bn Manchester Regt.)
12/5/1916   John Openshaw ( 6 Bn Cameron Highlanders)
25/5/1916   Joseph Hallworth (8 Bn South Lancashire Regt.)
1/7/1916    Frank Andrew Jackson ( 17 Bn Manchester Regt.)
3/7/1916    Harold Walters (11 Bn Cheshire Regt.)
14/7/1916   John William Marsland ( Royal Field Artillery)
15/7/1916   Walter Adshead (10 Bn Cheshire Regt.)
3/8/1916    Ernest Horace Dominick ( 6 Bn Cheshire Regt.)
11/8/1916   Arthur Daniels ( 8 Bn Cheshire Regt.)
18/8/1916   Frederick Rowbotham ( 12 Bn Kings Royal Rifle Corps.)
28/8/1916   Leonard Johnson ( 6 Bn Cheshire Regt.)
29/8/1916   Frederick Taylor ( 6 Bn Cheshire Regt.)
3/9/1916    Samuel Adshead ( 1 Bn Cameron Highlanders)
14/9/1916   Stanley Warburton ( 12 Bn Lancashire Fusiliers)
21/9/1916   Edwin Corbett ( Royal Garrison Artillery)
21/10/1916  Frank Clough ( 13 Bn Cheshire Regt.)
21/10/1916  William Poacher ( 8 Bn South Lancashire Regt.)
22/10/1916  Cuthbert Ashton ( 6 Bn Northumberland Fusiliers)
13/11/1916  Robert Bailey Fenna ( 6 Bn Cheshire Regt.)
13/11/1916  Frank Middlebrooke ( 6 Bn Cheshire Regt.)
21/11/1916  William Tierney ( 9 Bn Cheshire Regt.)
24/11/1916  John Grundey ( 9 Bn Cheshire Regt.)
28/11/1916  David Bennett ( 10 Bn Cheshire Regt.)
14/12/1916  Ernest Howe ( RAMC)

13/2/1917   Harold Percy King ( 1 Bn Kings Royal Lancaster Regt.)
21/3/1917   Albert Butterworth ( 63 Training Reserve Battalion)
14/4/1917   Ernest Dean ( 1 Bn Cheshire Regt.)
15/4/1917   George Arthur Vernon ( 5 Bn Royal Welch Fusiliers)
18/4/1917   Joseph Welbourn ( 15 Bn Cheshire Regt.)
3/5/1917    Bertram Clarke Stead ( 18 Bn Australian Imperial Force)
27/5/1917   Joseph Bannister ( 19 Bn Middlesex Regt.)
14/7/1917   Isaac Fidler ( 23 Bn Northumberland Fusiliers)

31/7/1917   Joseph Hallworth ( 6 Bn Cheshire Regt.)
3/8/1917    Herbert Hooley ( Royal Garrison Artillery)
9/8/1917    Abraham Mellor ( Royal Garrison Artillery)
19/8/1917   Samuel Daniels (16 Bn Cheshire Regt.)
23/8/1917   Charles Holebrook (14 Bn Welch Regt.)
1/9/1917    Herbert Gleave ( 11 Bn South Wales Borderers)
1/10/1917   Frederick Bennett ( Royal Field Artillery)
4/10/1917   James Swindells ( 22 Bn Manchester Regt.)
7/10/1917   George William Brown MM ( Royal Garrison Artillery)
9/10/1917   William Henry Bowers ( 10 Bn Cheshire Regt.)
9/10/1917   Arthur Henshall ( 2/6 Bn Lancashire Fusiliers)
9/10/1917   John Martin ( 1 Bn Cheshire Regt.)
11/10/1917  Harold Taylor ( 3 Bn Coldstream Guards)
12/10/1917  James Worthington ( Machine Gun Corps.)
25/10/1917  Allan Holebrook ( 1 Bn Cheshire Regt.)
25/10/1917  Percy Le Vesconte ( 1 Bn Cheshire Regt.)
10/11/1917  James Daniels ( 7th Bn Canadian Infantry Brigade -1st British Columbia)
15/11/1917  George Bancroft ( 2/6 Bn Lancashire Fusiliers)
14/12/1917  Walter Raymond Robinson ( 6 Bn Manchester Regt.)


10/1/1918   Stanley Clough ( 6 Bn Cheshire Regt.)
15/1/1918   Frederick Leah ( 9 Bn Welch Regt.)
21/3/1918   John Taylor ( Royal Garrison Artillery)
22/3/1918   William Hallworth ( 2 Bn South Lancashire Regt.)
22/3/1918   Harold Henshall ( Machine Gun Corps.)
22/3/1918   Walter Smith ( 11 Bn Lancashire Fusiliers)
24/3/1918   Frederick George Clarke (9 Bn Cheshire Regt.)
28/3/1918   Daniel Kilday ( 19 Bn Kings Liverpool Regt.)
9/4/1918    George Tallent ( 4 Bn South Lancashire Regt.)
10/4/1918   Norman Wilson (9 Bn Loyal North Lancashire Regt.)
13/4/1918   William Fidler (Royal Field Artillery)
15/4/1918   George Stubbs ( 2 Bn Duke of Wellington's Regt.)
24/4/1918   William Goodwin (Machine Gun Corps)
29/4/1918   Frank Hallam ( RASC)
10/5/1918   Winson Tallent ( Royal Field Artillery)
15/5/1918   Harold Skeen ( Machine Gun Corps)
19/5/1918   Robert Gee ( RAOC)
21/5/1918   Henry Barton Pillatt
30/5/1918   Frank Daniels ( 5 Bn South Wales Borderers)
31/5/1918   Gerald Griffiths (19 Bn Lancashire Fusiliers)
31/5/1918   Charles Johnson ( 9 Bn Cheshire Regt.)
7/6/1918    Ernest Marriott ( 2 Bn South Lancashire Regt.)
23/7/1918   Leonard Griffiths ( 6 Bn Seaforth Highlanders)
21/8/1918   Arnold Jones ( 7 Bn Kings Shropshire Light Infantry)
22/8/1918   Louis Brereton Jones ( 23 Bn Middlesex Regt.)
23/8/1918   Stanley Powell ( 12/13 Bn Northumberland Fusiliers)
2/9/1918    Ernest Clough ( 1 Bn Cheshire Regt.)
8/9/1918    Walter Ridgway (2 Bn Cheshire Regt.)

| | |
|---|---|
| 13/9/1918 | Reginald Hunt  (12 Bn Manchester Regt.) |
| 19/9/1918 | Henry Wood  ( 1 Bn Kings Shropshire Light Infantry) |
| 27/9/1918 | Arthur Eccles  (12/13 Bn Northumberland Fusiliers) |
| 28/9/1918 | Percy Oldham  ( 9 Bn Cheshire Regt.) |
| 29/9/1918 | Henry Bailey  ( 1 Bn Monmouthshire Regt.) |
| 29/9/1918 | John William Ridgway  ( Royal Field Artillery) |
| 10/10/1918 | Clifford Holt  ( 2 Bn Cheshire Regt.) |
| 14/10/1918 | George Wood  ( 4 Bn Cheshire Regt.) |
| 14/10/1918 | Edwin Young  ( 2 Bn South Wales Borderers) |
| 25/10/1918 | Reginald Holebrook  ( 4 Bn Cheshire Regt.) |
| 28/10/1918 | William Swindells  ( 10 Bn Northumberland Fusiliers) |
| 29/10/1918 | Edward Anthony Axon  ( 20 Bn Manchester Regt.) |
| 5/11/1918 | Harold Arthur Percival MM  ( 11 Bn Sherwood Foresters) |
| 8/11/1918 | Isaac Beeley  ( Machine Gun Corps.) |
| 28/11/1918 | James Daniels  ( RASC) |
| 15/12/1918 | Herbert Williamson  ( Depot Bn, Loyal North Lancashire Regt.) |
| 26/12/1918 | Charles Oldham  ( 14 Bn Royal Welch Fusiliers) |
| | |
| 19/2/1919 | Stephen Wynn Vickers MC  DFC  ( 200 Sqdn RAF) |
| 22/6/1919 | John Malpass  ( 2 Bn North Staffordshire Regt.) |
| 20/7/1919 | Edward Hammond Taylor  (Cameronians) |
| | |
| 13/3/1920 | Roland Bailey |
| 28/4/1920 | James Pilsbury  ( 15 Bn Cheshire Regt.) |
| 31/7/1920 | Edward Painter  ( Royal Field Artillery) |
| 26/11/1920 | George Ridgway  ( RASC) |
| | |
| 19/9/1925 | Frank Johnson  ( Kings Own Royal Lancaster Regt.) |
| | |
| 17/5/1939 | John Henry Clarke  ( 2 Bn Cheshire Regt.) |
| | |
| 31/8/1943 | James Hammond Hallworth  ( 3rd Canadian Mounted Regt.) |

Dates not known - Frederick Bann
                       Arthur Cooper
                       Harold Phillips

~~~~~

# S21037 Private Samuel **Adshead**
## 1st Bn. Queen's Own Cameron Highlanders
## 3 September 1916

On 15 October 1915 the Stockport Advertiser, in its "Hazel Grove News" section, reported that Samuel Adshead, together with John Openshaw and John Brown, had enlisted and left the village for training.

Samuel and his wife Catherine had two children, Catherine (born 5 March 1913) and Winifred (born 16 November 1914) but, later described as being "high spirited", Samuel could not resist the lure of the Colours. Not for Samuel and his friends the mundaneness of joining the local regiment - The Cheshires. It had to be something more romantic and exciting. So when they enlisted in Stockport on 7 October, they decided to join the Queen's Own Cameron Highlanders. It was therefore to Inverness that they set off on that October day. Sadly, neither Samuel nor John Openshaw survived their great adventure and the paper even reported on 7 September 1917 that all three of them had been killed, pointing out the fact they had enlisted together. Fortunately for John Brown, it was wrong.

Samuel was born on 28 June 1890, the son of John and Jane Adshead of 103 Commercial Road, and was baptised at Norbury Church on 12 October of that year. John was a spinner in one of the local mills.

Samuel himself became a bleacher and was 25 years 90 days old and 5 feet 5 inches tall when he enlisted. He lived with his wife and two children at 109 Commercial Road, just three houses away from his parents.His main hobby was football, and he was said to have regularly been seen "engaged in the winter pastime".

After a short spell of training he was posted to the 1st Battalion, which was a regular battalion before the war, and all too soon he arrived at the front. His spell of life in the Army was however dreadfully short, for less than eleven months after he enlisted he was dead, aged 26.

The First Battalion was engaged in the bitter fighting of the Battle of the Somme. Whilst we have no record confirming it, his length of service makes it likely that Samuel was not involved in the first days of the battle, but was drafted in shortly afterwards to replace those killed in the horrific days of July.

On Sunday 3 September 1916 the 1st Battalion, which was one of the three battalions that formed the 1st Division of the 1st Brigade of the British Army, attacked Wood Lane which was near High Wood, with a detachment of the 8th Berkshire Regiment on their right. During the day the temperature rose to 72 degrees F. and there was a slight fall of rain of about 4mm. The fighting was bitter and no progress was made on the right. The Camerons however, were successful and they managed to continue for another 100 yards before stopping to consolidate.

At 3pm. the Germans made a determined counter attack of considerable ferocity and the battalion was forced back to its starting line. Some time during the fighting, Samuel Adshead disappeared.

At first there was hope. His body had not been found and he was reported missing, but in June 1917 the Authorities decided that there was no choice but to officially declare him dead.

His body was never found and he is commemorated, along with 73000 others who have no known grave and who died in the area of the Battle of the Somme, on the Thiepval Memorial near Albert in France. Eight Hazel Grove men have their names inscribed on that monument. Samuel's name is also on the memorial of Hazel Grove Congregational Church which is now in the United Reformed Church in Short Street.

~~~~

# 35234  Private Walter **Adshead**
## 10th Bn. Cheshire Regiment
## 15 July 1916
(Picture)

To receive any official message regarding your son who is away at the front is not likely to be a be a welcome occasion, particularly when the letter is partially mutilated and you cannot therefore read it fully. This happened to John Adshead of 76 Chapel Street around the middle of July 1916.

What could be deciphered was bad enough, because it indicated that his son Walter had been wounded during what later became known as the Battle of the Somme. The nature of the injury was not stated and little else could be made out.

Two weeks later, in the first week of August, John Adshead received a letter from one of Walter's comrades informing him that his son had died and that the writer had been a member of the burial party. The letter also said that the wound was such that death must have been instantaneous, which does not really fit in with the official notification of his having been wounded. Perhaps it was a friend trying to let the parents down gently by saying that he had not suffered. It was a common theme of such communications. The letter went on to say that Walter had been interred on the field of battle (which would not have happened if he had been wounded and been taken to a Casualty Station before dying), so it is possible that he had first been wounded but within a few days went back into the line where, shortly after, he was killed . We will never know.

Walter Adshead, according to the Stockport Advertiser, enlisted on 15 February but no year is given. One can only assume that it was the same year - 1916 - in which case his period of service lasted only five months. He had worked at Hollins Mill before he joined up, and had had hopes of "improving his position". He also had a brother in the Army.

Although it missed the first day of the Battle of the Somme, the 10th Battalion was in the trenches and involved in the battle from the 2nd until the 15th of July. It was on this last day that Walter is said to have been killed.

The battalion was in front of the town of Ovillers and the History of the Cheshire Regiment states that it had "a very sticky time". On Friday the 14th it took part in an attack near Bazentin, under heavy fire which meant that the men had to crawl up the slope to the German trenches, the slope being completely swept by fire. The battalion was nearly destroyed in this attack but despite this, they were ordered to attack again at 2.50 am on the 15th. As dawn broke the air was misty but during the morning it cleared to become a bright day with the temperature rising to 72F. It is doubtful that Walter Adshead lived to see it, as most of the casualties occured in the first few hours of the day.

There was no artillery support and the battalion's attack was mainly carried out by bombing their way forward. They nearly reached their objective, but heavy machine gun fire forced the remaining men to withdraw and 14 officers and 366 men became casualties.

Walter Adshead is buried in Pozieres British Cemetery, Ovillers-La Boisselle, France, which is on the road from Albert to Bapaume. His grave is in Plot II , Row F , Grave 32. In addition, he is commemorated on the War Memorials at the Methodist Church and Stockport Art Gallery.

~~~~~

# 5050 Private Cuthbert **Ashton**
## 6th Bn Northumberland Fusiliers
## 22 October 1916

There was no report in any of the local newspapers when Cuthbert Ashton died of wounds in France on 22 October 1916, though the Stockport Advertiser did have a small paragraph in its 7 January 1916 edition stating that he was one of six brothers in the Army. At that time he was stationed in Morpeth.

The date was before the introduction of conscription (10 February 1916), so clearly he had made a positive choice to join the Northumberland Fusiliers though we do not now know the reason. Perhaps one or more of his brothers was in the regiment.

Born on 26 March 1897, he lived at 31 Station Street and before joining up he was a porter/shunter for the London and North Western Railway at Stockport. It would appear that he had found it difficult to find a job that suited him, because on 20 January 1913, at the age of 15, he had started as an apprentice in the Fitting Department at Mirrlees, having previously been 'at trade'. The job was not to his liking - he left on 25 March 1913. His father Stephen, gave his occupation was given as 'Retired Doctor'. As a child he had been a religious boy because on 23 September 1903 and again on 27 September 1905 he was specially mentioned by the Headmaster in the Norbury School Log book, for his examination results in Religious Knowledge.

The 6th Battalion was a Territorial battalion and Cuthbert enlisted in it in Newcastle upon Tyne, despite living in Hazel Grove. Like many other battalions at the time, it had been heavily involved in the Battle of the Somme and it was still engaged in the tail end of that battle when Cuthbert died.

From the 1st to the 3rd October 1916 the battalion was in support in the trenches and was then moved into reserve where they underwent training courses and provided men for numerous working parties. From 16 to 20 October they provided men for night operations, digging forward trenches, and as he died of wounds on 22 October, it is distinctly possible that Cuthbert Ashton was wounded in one of these operations.

Cuthbert is buried in Etretat Churchyard, Seine-Maritime, France, in Plot II, Row B, Grave 15. He was aged 19.

Not only is he commemorated on the Memorial in Norbury Church, but he is also on the Roll of Honour of London and NW Railwaymen, a large volume published after the war by the company, which listed all the employees of the company who had been killed together with their precise occupation and place of work.

~~~~~

# 40514  Private Edward Anthony **Axon**
## 20th Bn. Manchester Regiment
## 29 October 1918
(Picture)

"Teddy", as he was known to his friends, was the son of Thomas E. and Mary A. Axon of 22 Argyle Street, and before joining up on 28 October 1915 he was employed at the Stockport Co-operative Society at their Starr Inn Stores. Before that he worked at   N. Gould's stores in Shaw Heath. His father was a hatter.

Throughout his life he was a regular attender at both the Hazel Grove Wesleyan Sunday School and Chapel.  At his death he was 24 years of age and left behind a fiancee, Alice, who lived in Park Lane, Poynton.

Originally, Teddy enlisted in Chester, even though he was living in Hazel Grove, and joined the Cheshire Yeomanry but, along with most Yeomanry Regiments, this was disbanded during the war and its members transferred to other regiments. The fact that he took the trouble to go to Chester to enlist suggests that he specifically wanted to join the Yeomanry. He went to France first and then in November 1917 went to Italy. Whilst there, he saved two soldiers from drowning in the River Pivan. Six weeks before he died, he returned to France, where he was attached to Headquarters.

He nearly survived the war, but it was not enemy action that killed him, rather the influenza pandemic which swept the world in 1918. Teddy contracted pneumonia and whilst laid low with that, he caught influenza. It only took three days to kill him.

When the pneumonia took hold, he was taken to hospital in Rouen and is buried in St. Sever Cemetery Extension, Rouen, Block S, Plot II, Row K, Grave 7 and is also commemorated on the Memorial at the Methodist Church. John Grundey, who died two years earlier, is also buried in the cemetery.

~~~~~

# 2nd. Lieutenant Geoffrey Hamilton **Bagshawe**
## 1st Bn Royal Dragoon Guards
## 13 May 1915
(Picture)

The elder son of Ernest and Frances Alice Devereux Bagshawe of Poise House, his original name was Carver and he was killed at Hooge, just outside Ypres, on 13 May 1915.

Ernest Carver was the grandson of the founder of the Hollins Mill Co of Portland Street, Manchester, Marple and Hazel Grove and was the son of Thomas Carver, prominent in Manchester in connection with the City Mission. By 1914 he had become the Managing Director of the company, but previously he was the manager of the Wellington Mill, which was on the site now occupied by the Pemberton Packaging Company. On 23 January 1899, Ernest was elected as a manager of Norbury School and continued in that role for many years, being instrumental in bringing about a much needed extension to the building in January 1914.

Ernest's wife, Alice, was the daughter of Mr. W.H. Greaves-Bagshawe D.L. of Ford Hall, Chapel en le Frith and, in March 1914, after the death of his father in law, Ernest and his wife inherited Ford Hall and changed their name by Royal Licence to Bagshawe. So did their children.

Born in Poynton on 24 June 1889, Geoffrey was baptised at St. George's Church, Poynton on 6 August 1889 whilst living at 'Westfield', Poynton. His father's occupation is given as 'Gentleman', but when his younger brother, Francis Ernest Gisborne Carver was baptised at the same church on 26 October 1893, his father was shown as a Cotton Manufacturer of Poise House, Torkington. Geoffrey was sent away early to Boarding School and was educated at Stone House, Broadstairs, Harrow School and Christ Church, Oxford. Whilst at Oxford, he was a member of the OTC and, on taking his degree, was nominated a University candidate for the Army.

He was gazetted to the 1st Royal Dragoons in February 1911 and joined the regiment in South Africa. In 1913 he left the Army to take up farming in Rhodesia, but on the outbreak of war returned to England where he was offered a temporary commission as a 2nd Lieutenant in his old regiment in September 1914. The following month he went to Flanders where, on 12 November, he was wounded in the leg by a piece of shrapnel and was invalided home.

Returning to the front in April 1915, he rejoined his regiment. Ypres was feared throughout the British Army as it was a small salient which, for political reasons, was to be defended at all costs. A salient was a part of the line of trenches which jutted out into the enemy lines. In this case, it extended from two or three miles north of Ypres, a similar distance all round the east and south of the town. It had no military significance and, being a salient, could be and was shelled constantly from three sides. Hooge was at the apex of the salient and was fought over continually for the whole duration of the war, being won and lost many times. Hooge was one of the worst places in the worst sector of the war and it was there that Geoffrey was killed on 13 May 1915, aged 25, the third death of the war from Hazel Grove.

At about 4am a tremendous bombardment rained down on the Royals, the heaviest they had so far experienced in the war and even though they were in the support trenches, rather than the front line itself, they suffered considerable casualties. At about 7am the message came to them that the line of the 3rd Dragoons had been broken so they made their way up to support them. Unfortunately the message proved to be incorrect but whilst returning to their trenches the Royals were caught in the open by another barrage. Again there were heavy casualties.

The news of Geoffrey's death was sent by telegram to the Police Station at Hazel Grove,and arrived on the night of Saturday 15 May, but the family were in London. The policeman therefore informed the gardener Mr. Johnson, and he had the task of informing the family.

Being a prominent family in the district, and also because the flood of deaths had not yet started, the family received much sympathy from the people of the village. At the evening service on 23 May the vicar, when reading out, as he regularly did, the "Roll of Honour" of 93 names of those currently serving their King and Country, especially singled out the name of 2nd Lieut. Bagshawe for mention and announced that on behalf of both himself and the congregation he had written to the parents expressing his deep sympathy. Geoffrey was well known among the employees of Hollins Mill .

A senior officer of the regiment wrote to Ernest Bagshawe saying-
"In your son we have lost as good a troop leader as there ever was in the Regiment, absolutely cool and undisturbed under the most trying circumstances, knowing not the meaning of the word fear; well loved and rightly, highly esteemed and deeply regretted by officers and all ranks of the Regiment. He has died a gallant death, in a good and just cause - and I can only say I most deeply regret him as a friend and as an invaluable officer. We, alas, lost heavily in the Regiment - out of 340 all ranks, there remained this morning I believe, 180. The general told me tonight they fought gallantly, and that is the only point we can be thankful for. May we in our turn do as well".

Geoffrey's death was fairly early on in the conflict and his grave was soon lost. He therefore has no known grave and is commemorated on the Menin Gate at Ypres, along with 55,000 other men who died in the salient between the beginning of the war and 15 August 1917 and have no known grave. Four other Hazel Grove men are similarly commemorated. In addition there are 35,000 names on the Memorial at Tyne Cot Cemetery for men who died in the salient between 15 August 1917 and the end of the war and have no known grave. There are 10 Hazel Grove men on that Memorial.

Geoffrey Bagshawe is also commemorated on the Memorials in Norbury Church and Harrow School. His younger brother Francis Ernest Gisborne Bagshawe, served as a Lieutenant in 1st Lancashire Yeomanry, attached to 9th Tank Corps, and survived the war. Ernest's two sons in law where in the Royal Navy, one having been involved in the Battle of the Falkland Isles in December 1914.

~~~~~

# 12252  Private Frederick **Bailey**
## 1st Bn. Cheshire Regiment
## 25 June 1915

The 1st Battalion Cheshire Regiment was a regular battalion, but Frederick Bailey worked at Christy's Hatworks in Stockport before the war, so he must have been a replacement drafted in from the recently recruited volunteers to fill up the gaps left by earlier casualties.

The son of Walter and Harriet Bailey of 34 Peter Street, he was born in Hazel Grove and was 24 when he was killed in action on 25 June 1915. His father was an overlooker in a local mill and Frederick enlisted into the Cheshire Regiment in Stockport.

Being a regular battalion, the 1st Cheshires took a lot of the early strain of war before the new "Kitchener" battalions, made up virtually completely of volunteers from the first few months of recruiting after the war started, could be fully trained and sent out into action. From the 24 May to 30 June 1915, the battalion was in the trenches outside Ypres for 38 continuous days, holding a line in front of Zillebeke, just south of Hill 60.

They had four companies, rotating so that each company served twelve days at the front and four days in reserve. The line itself was, at the time, comparatively quiet, but every morning and every evening the trenches were heavily bombarded by the German artillery in periods known as the morning and evening "hates". Snipers were also very active and caused many casualties. During this "tour", the first Zeppelin reached England, and on returning it passed directly over the Cheshires early one morning.

Throughout the period, the weather was very good, but the trenches were very open and gave little protection from either shell or sniper fire. During one of the "hates" on the second day of their spell in the front line, heavy shellfire killed a number of men, and several, including Frederick, disappeared. Despite the fact that he was one of the village's earlier casualties, there was no mention of his death in the local newspapers.

Originally, Frederick was posted as missing, as he is so shown on a Roll of Honour published by the Wesleyan Church on 13 December 1915. This gave details of all the young men of its congregation who had gone off to fight in the war. Some time later, the decision was taken to officially list him as having been killed. The Menin Gate in Ypres contains Frederick's name as he has no known grave. He is also commemorated on the Memorials at the Methodist Church, Christy's Hatworks and Stockport Art Gallery.

~~~~

# 316264 Private Henry **Bailey**
## 1st Bn Monmouthshire Regiment
## 29 September 1918

Whether Henry Bailey ever lived in Hazel Grove is not clear, but his grandmother, uncle and sister did, at 5 Smithy Street. In the circumstances, they no doubt put his name on the list for inclusion on the Memorial.

Henry was born in Hull and was the son of Henry and Mary Jane Bailey of 122 Newbridge Lane, Stockport. He enlisted in Stockport into the 4th Battalion of the Monmouthshire Regiment but this was a reserve battalion which provided drafts for the various battalions of the regiment serving in France. Henry was serving with the 1st Battalion when he was killed, aged 21, on 29 September 1918.

 The battalion was acting as the pioneer battalion for the Division as it contained many South Wales miners who were considered ideal for this type of work, and an attack was made between Bellenglise and Riqueval in order to cross the St. Quentin canal . The canal itself was approximately 30 metres wide and immediately behind it was the Hindeburg Line, a massive line of  fortifications erected by the Germans some time before to cover the possibility of their having to withdraw. They had had plenty of time to prepare it and had done so with typical thoroughness.

A and B companies were employed carrying cork pier bridges and superstructures up to the canal and these were to be erected immediately after the attacking infantry had crossed . As the massive British barrage opened up at 5.50am , thick fog descended making it very difficult to see what was going on. Despite this, the bridging material was brought up on time.

By the afternoon, the battalion had bridged the canal and were involved in repairing the road from Bellenglise to Joncourt as part of the consolidation work. During the day, 30 casualties were suffered as the work was carried out under heavy shell and machine gun fire. Presumably, Henry was one of these.

Henry Bailey is buried in Vadencourt British Cemetery, Maissemy, France, in Plot1, Row B, Grave 12, and is also commemorated on the Memorial at Stockport Art Gallery.

~~~~~

# Roland **Bailey**
## 13 March 1920

 Just two short lines in the Death Notice columns of both the Stockport Advertiser and Stockport Express are the only mentions in the local papers of the existence of Roland Bailey. Although he died within the time limits used by the Commonwealth War Graves Commission, they have no trace of him.

The announcements merely stated that Roland had died on 13 March 1920 at 3, Cook Street, Stockport, aged 35 years. There is no mention of his regiment, war service or even of family, but his Death Certificate gives a clue that this is the man whose name is on the War Memorial. In addition, he was buried in Norbury Churchyard.

Born at 8, Harrop's Yard, Hazel Grove in 1885, he was the son of John Bailey a bleacher's winder, and his wife Mary. The 1891 Census shows him to be 6 years old and their only child at that time, but by 1907 there is no trace of the family in the village. In 1920 however, Mary was a widow and was back in the village, living at 61, London Road (now part of the site of Wynsor's Shoe Store).

Nothing more can be traced until his death on 13 March 1920 at 3, Cook Sreet, Stockport. This is a small street off King Street, Stockport, opposite the Bus Station in Daw Bank. His wife reported the death but only her initial - C. is given. Roland was a pavior's labourer, and he died of heart disease brought on by malaria. This is the clue that this is the correct man. Malaria would have been contracted whilst abroad, probably in the Middle East or East Africa, and in those days the only real opportunity that most working people would have had to go to such places would have been whilst serving in the forces.

Roland Bailey was buried in the family grave, E261, at Norbury Churchyard on 16 March 1920. If there ever was a gravestone, it no longer exists and the grave is now simply a patch of grass.

~~~~~

# 242382 Private George **Bancroft**
## 2/6th Bn Lancashire Fusiliers
## 15 November 1917

For a number of years, George Bancroft had been a volunteer in the Territorials, with the result that he was fairly quickly called to the Colours after the start of the war. On 23 November 1914 he left the village to join the 6th Battalion of the Cheshire Regiment in Chester. He was also a long time member of the Mechanics Institute and therefore, on the day he left, the members made a presentation to him of a Smoking Cabinet. The presentation was made by Mr. Arnfield of the Institute and George thanked them with a few "characteristic" remarks.

The only traces of a 'George Bancroft' that can be found, are those shown in the 1891 Census, a 'Hatter Planker' aged 26, living on London Road, Stockport Moor (the row of cottages between the George & Dragon and Poplar Grove). No actual number is given and if this is the same man, he would have been 43 when he joined up, and about 46 when he was killed. It was not impossible, but very unusual for a man of that age to be in the Army. The other traces are the1907 and 1910 Hazel Grove Directories which show a person of the same name at 56,Commercial Road. He was a 'mill hand'.

Little else can be found out about him, The Commonwealth War Graves Commision have no details of his next of kin, but at some time he must have been transferred to the 2nd/6th Battalion of the Lancashire Fusiliers because he was serving with them at the end of the Battle of Passchendaele when he was killed in action on 15 November 1917. In fact the battle had actually drawn to a close a few days before. The mud was so thick and deep that men were unable to walk through it, they dragged themselves inch by inch and step by weary step taking five minutes to travel a few feet. The rain had hardly stopped for weeks and the cold paralysed the men, draining away their will to go on.

On the 15th November the battalion was holding the line near Broodseinde (outside Ypres) where they had been when the battle died out a few days before. It could hardly be said to be a strongpoint. A series of water and mud-filled shell holes into which men could, and did, slip, never to be seen again, was a more accurate description. George, however, has a grave, so he must have been killed by a sniper or shell fire rather than just disappeared into the mud.

George Bancroft lies in Dochy Farm New British Cemetery, Langemark, Belgium, in Plot III, Row D, Grave 10. It was at Langemark, on 22 April 1915 (two and a half years before), that the Germans first released poison gas against the Allies.

~~~~

# Frederick W **Bann**
(Picture)

The name of Frederick Bann was not on the first list of names to be inscribed on the War Memorial when the Stockport Advertiser published the list on 20 July 1923, but his name was included on the Memorial when it was unveiled on the 11th November of that year. Clearly, someone put his name forward in the intervening period and the War Memorial Committee accepted it as being valid.

The problem is that his name is not held by The Commonwealth War Graves Commission as being a casualty of the war between 1914 and 1921. The CWGC's records include all members of Colonial and Commonwealth forces as well as those of Great Britain. Neither is it on the Registrar General's list of deaths, either civil or military, between 1914 and the end of 1923.

In his book 'The History of Hazel Grove', D.H.Trowsdale mentions a cricket team of 1910, whose members were all Hazel Grove butchers. One of the team members is 'Fred Bann - who was at Hazel Grove CWS and later went abroad'. Unfortunately, he does not say where this information came from or what country Fred went to. The Stockport Advertiser of 31 July 1903 states that in a game of cricket a few days before, between the 'Butchers' and the 'Grocers' of Hazel Grove, the captain of the 'Butchers' team was Frederick Bann.

The U.S. Army have no trace of a casualty by that name and therefore, unless he went to a non English speaking country, it may be that he died of wounds or illness in Australia, Canada, South Africa, the USA or some similar country after the CWGC records were compiled in 1921 but before the War Memorial was erected in 1923.

The 1891 Census shows Frederick Bann, a butcher aged 18, living at 184, London Road (now Bannister, Preston & Ormerod), with his mother Harriett, a 50 year old widow and with his aunt and uncle, Josiah and Sarah Gosling. If this is the same man, then he would have been in his forties when he died. The 1907 Hazel Grove Directory shows a 'Fred Bann', millhand at 88 and 90, Commercial Road, but the Street Directory for that address states him to be - 'a fish and chip dealer'. The 1910 Directory shows him to be a butcher at 9, Cooper Street.

In addition to the War Memorial, Frederick Bann's name is also on the Congregational Church Memorial at the United Reformed Church.

~~~~

# 2458 Private Joseph **Bannister**
## 19th Bn Middlesex Regiment
## 27 May 1917
(Picture)

Beatrice Yard was a small row of three houses behind and between 188 and 190 London Road, (currently William Hill's and the Vernon Building Society) and Joseph Bannister's brother Amos, who was a labourer, lived there at number 6 with his wife Mary. Amos is given as Joseph's next of kin in the CWGC records which were compiled in 1921, but at the time of his death Joseph appears to have been living with his sister at 11, Richard Street, Stockport. He never married.

Joseph was born in Hazel Grove and enlisted in Chester, even though he still lived in Hazel Grove. The 1891 Census shows him to be living at 1, Warren Court, (immediately next to Beatrice Yard) with his parents Joseph, a coal miner and Sarah Jane, as well as his two brothers and two sisters. Joseph was 3 years old and his brother Amos was19.

He enlisted in the Middlesex Regiment at the beginning of the war, and prior to joining up he was employed by a Manchester builder and contractor named Worthington.

On 27 May 1917, when Joseph was killed in action, the 19th Battalion was fighting near the Messines - Wytschaete Ridge, outside Ypres. The Battle of Messines, which was a preliminary to the Third Battle of Ypres, started a few days later, so it is likely that the regiment was in the front line preparing for the forthcoming battle. There are no details of exactly how he was killed.

Joseph Bannister is buried in Dickebusch New Military Cemetery Extension, near Ypres, Belgium, in Plot III, Row A, Grave 11. He is also commemorated on the Memorials at the Methodist Church and at Stockport Art Gallery. He was 29 years old.

~~~~~~

# 7064 Private William George **Bartlett**
## 1st Bn Cheshire Regiment
## 13 October 1914

When William Bartlett was killed in action near Festubert in France on 13 October 1914, he became the first Hazel Grove serviceman to die in the Great War. He was 32 years old.

William was born in Kennington, London, but sometime later his mother, Sarah, married James Hatton, a collier, and moved to 42, Brook Sreet, Hazel Grove. There is no indication that William ever married.

The 1st Battalion, Cheshire Regiment was a regular battalion and as William was killed only two months after the outbreak of war, it is almost certain that he was a regular soldier. The local papers made no mention of his death, but as he enlisted in Stockport, it would seem that he had probably lived in the village for some time.

The 1st Battalion was very quickly thrown into the fray, and was soon involved in the desperate attempts to stem the German invasion of Belgium and France and their efforts to reach the Channel ports thus cutting off the British Army from its line of retreat. In what was called "the Race for the sea", each side tried to outflank the other and reach the Channel ports first. This desperate race lasted from 10 October to 2 November, but William lost his life after only three days of it.

The 1st Battalion was part of 11 Corps. who were given the task of turning the German flank and on Monday 12 October they took up a line covering Festubert, with Givenchy on the battalion's left. At dawn on the 13th the Cheshires sent two strong patrols out towards a large farmstead called Chapelle St. Roch which was part of the village of Rue D'Ouvert. William would appear to have been in one of these patrols. They managed to occupy the farm and after fighting all day, the enemy were all around them. The Germans set light to the outbuildings and haystacks and only a few men remained unwounded. The survivors were forced to surrender, but Willam was not among them and his grave, if he ever had one, has never been found.

As a result, he has no known grave and is therefore commemorated on the Memorial at Le Touret, just south of the road between Bethune and Armentieres in France. His name is also on the Memorial at Norbury Church.

~~~~

# 169454 Private Isaac **Beeley**
## 19 Squadron, Machine Gun Corps(Cavalry)
## 8 November 1918

Isaac Beeley was probably in the Territorial Army before the war because the records show that he enlisted in Stockport in the 5th Reserve Cavalry Regiment, which was a Territorial Regiment. At some time he transferred into The Machine Gun Corps and , being a cavalryman, was placed in the cavalry section.

Before he joined up, Isaac, who was born in Hazel Grove, had married Eleanor Heywood, and is shown in the 1910 Hazel Grove Directory as being a heating engineer, living at 2, Mount Pleasant. His father George was also a heating engineer, living at 17 Bramhall Moor Lane. All we know of his mother is that her initials were "S.E."

No mention of Isaac's death can be traced in the local papers so we can find out little else about him. 19 Squadron was formed in Palestine in June 1917 and the records show that it left there for France in May 1918. Isaac must however have become ill at some time before then, because he remained behind and died in Cairo on 8 November 1918. There is no record of precisely what his illness was. He was 32 years old.

Isaac Beeley is buried in Cairo War Memorial Cemetery, in Plot M, Grave 199, and he is also commemorated on the memorial at the Methodist Church. After the War, his widow Eleanor lived at 4 Willard Street.

~~~~~

# 49139 Private David **Bennett**
## 10th Bn Cheshire Regiment
## 28 November 1916

Samuel and Elizabeth Bennett lost two sons in The Great War, David being the first to die.His brother Frederick followed him 10 months later.David was born in Hazel Grove at 33 Nelson Street, but when The Commonwealth War Graves Commission records were compiled in 1921, their address is given as 21 Nelson Street.

The 10th Battalion of The Cheshire Regiment was involved in The Battle of the Somme and David Bennett survived this. The last real action of the battle, which started on 1 July 1916, was on 14 November 1916. By then, thousands upon thousands of men, on both sides, had been killed and the battle had ground to a halt in the mud, rain and despair that encompassed that shattered landscape, just as the Third Battle of Ypres was to do, a few miles to the north, almost exactly a year later.

The 10th Battalion had fought in the battle to secure the heights above the River Ancre at the northern end of the Somme battlefield and were still there on 28 November 1916, when David was killed in action. They were garrisoning a former German strongpoint called "Stuff Redoubt", and at the same time had companies "carrying" for other Brigades.The Battalion War Diary states that there were no casualties between 25 November and 1 December, but other official records quite clearly state that David was killed in action on 28 November.

David Bennett is commemorated on  the Ploegsteert Memorial in Belgium which is a considerable distance from where his battalion was on the day he is alleged to have been killed in action. It would appear that he was not actually with them when he died, so presumably he was one of the men 'carrying' for other Brigades.

He is also commemorated on the Congregational Church Memorial which is now situated in The United Reformed Church in Short Street.

~~~~~

## 43727 Driver Frederick **Bennett**
## "D" Battery, 190 Brigade Royal Field Artillery
## 1 October 1917

When their son David was killed on 28 November 1916, Samuel and Elizabeth Bennett must have worried more than normally about their other son Frederick. Sadly, their worries came true all too soon, for he died of wounds only 10 months later.

Frederick was born at 33 Nelson Street on 12 March 1895, his father Samuel being a spinner in one of the local mills. He was baptised at Norbury Church on 13 August 1899 with his sister Martha, who was born on 4 October 1890. At some time later his parents moved to 21, Nelson Street.

No details are available of his occupation prior to joining up, but he was living in West Ham, London when he joined the Royal Field Artillery and like his brother, his death was not reported in the local newspapers.

Whatever his wounds were, it was possible to get him to hospital because he died behind the lines, and is buried in Lijssenthoek Military Cemetery which is two miles south of Poperinghe in Belgium. Poperinghe itself is four or five miles west of Ypres. Frederick Bennett was 22 years old when he died and is buried in Plot XXV, Row E, Grave 18A. Number 17 Casualty Clearing Station was in the area at the time and it is therefore highly likely that that is where he died. George Brown, also from Hazel Grove, died at that Clearing Station only six days later and is buried in the same cemetery.

In addition, like his brother, he is commemorated on the Congregational Church Memorial, which is now in the United Reformed Church, Short Street.

~~~~~

# 12123 Sergeant William Henry **Bowers**
## 10th Bn Cheshire Regiment
## 9 October 1917
(Picture)

Harry Bowers was born in Poynton, but must have been living in Hazel Grove when he joined the Cheshire Regiment, because on 4 November 1917 a special Memorial Service was held at the Primitive Methodist Church for two members of the Church who had recently been killed on active service. In fact, they both died on the same day. Harry was one and the other was John Martin. Both had been members of the Church and its Sunday School. Arthur Henshall also died on that day, but presumably he was not a Primitive Methodist and so did not get a mention. Both the 1907 and 1910 Hazel Grove Directories show a William Bowers at 17, Grosvenor Street.

The Primitive Methodist Church was situated on London Road right next to the open ground upon which, six years later, was to be built the Hazel Grove War Memorial commemorating both of them and their fellow comrades.

There is some confusion regarding the records of Harry's death. The Battalion War Diary states that the Battalion was near Ypres on 9 October 1917 and that it was a quiet day spent digging an extension to a trench. There were no casualties, it says.

However, the official records state that Harry was killed in action and what makes it more confusing is that he was buried near Bethune in France, about 25 miles away from Ypres. No doubt this made little difference to his young wife. It seems most likely that Harry was wounded earlier and the battalion moved after this to Ypres where, at the time, the Third Battle of Ypres was raging. Alternatively, he may have been attached to another regiment, although this is normally made clear in the records.

William Henry Bowers is buried at Gorre British and Indian Cemetery, Beauvry, near Bethune in France, in Plot IV, Row E, Grave 22. After the war, his wife left Hazel Grove to live at 32 Hawkins Street, South Reddish. He is also commemorated on the Memorials at the Methodist Church and at Stockport Art Gallery. Walter Robinson, who died two months later, is buried in the same cemetery.

~~~~~

# 123985 Gunner George William **Brown M.M.**
## 23 Siege Battery, Royal Garrison Artillery
## 7 October 1917
(Picture)

George Brown was, before the war, widely known in Stockport footballing circles. For many years he was connected with the Stockport Junior Football League as well as being a member of the Stockport and District Sunday School League. He didn't confine his activities just to playing either. He was both a member and assistant secretary of the Stockport F.A.. The interest ran in the family, as his father was the treasurer and vice president of the Stockport F.A.

He was married to Mary Duncan Brown and they had two children. The Stockport Advertiser of 19 October 1917 gave his home address as 35 Katherine Road, Stockport, whereas the Advertiser of 26 October gave it as 10, Catherine Street, Stockport. His parents, John and Mary Brown, lived at 'Sunbeam', 25, Commercial Road, as did his sisters.

George had been called up about 12 months before his death and had been serving at the front for only about 4 months. In that short time he had distinguished himself enough to be awarded the Military Medal after his death. The award was announced in the London Gazette of 17 December 1917, but unlike other medals, no citation was given for the MM. Sometimes the medal was given for extremely good soldiering and sometimes for acts of gallantry, and regretfully we now have no way of knowing the reason for the award. The Royal Artillery have no records which throw light on it. Equally, because of its sheer size, it cannot give details of where each particular gun team was at any given time, so it is not possible to find out the circumstances surrounding his death.

A memorial service was held at the Congregational Church on Sunday 21 October 1917, when the Rev. G.M. Jenkins made reference both to George Brown and to other members of the congregation who had been killed. A Miss Ellerby sang a solo specially for the occasion and Mr. Mercer, the organist, played 'O rest in the Lord' "to great effect".

George Brown died of wounds at 17 Casualty Clearing Station on 7 October 1917, during the Third Battle of Ypres, and is buried at Lijssenthoek Military Cemetery, Belgium, in Plot XX, Row I, Grave 15. He was 35 years old. In addition, his name is on the Congregational Church section of the Memorial in the United Reformed Church and on the Memorial at Stockport Art Gallery. After his death, his wife and children went to live at 37, Gore Street, Gorton, though it is thought that his daughter married and lived in Hazel Grove for many years until she died in the 1980's. Frederick Bennett, who died six days earlier, is buried in the same cemetery.

~~~~~

# 9982 Private Joseph **Burgess**
## 2nd Bn Cheshire Regiment
## 3 October 1915

Born in Hazel Grove in 1895, Joseph Burgess was a regular soldier who married Elizabeth Ann Hallworth, aged 17, at Norbury Church on 30 November 1914. At the time he was living with his mother at Clock Cottage, Norbury, but between then and when Joseph was killed on 3 October 1915, aged 20, his mother had moved to 31, Brentnall Street, Stockport. There is no information as to what happened to Elizabeth Ann.

Like many other regular battalions, the 2nd Cheshires had a hard time during the first twelve months of the war. The History of The Cheshire Regiment tells us that at the beginning of October 1915, the battalion was involved in the heavy fighting of the Battle of Loos and were in front of the southern portion of an extremely well fortified German strongpoint named the "Hohenzollern Redoubt". Due to constant bombardment and heavy fighting, the trenches were in a very bad state and Major Roddy, the C.O., advised HQ that no further attacks should take place.

Brigade either failed to realise just how bad conditions were, or simply ignored the message, and ordered attack after attack, despite their continued failure. The troops were bombed all day and had such heavy casualties that they became very disorganised in the maze of badly damaged trenches.

The Germans attacked on 3 October and were repulsed on most of the line except the left, where they gained a footing. All the Cheshires' bombers were killed. The battalion then made a bayonet counter attack, but was met with a hail of bombs and was driven back. Later in the morning, the Germans attacked again, sweeping in from the left where they had gained their earlier foothold and the Cheshires were driven back. The defenders had reached the limits of their endurance.

Six officers and 43 men were killed, seven officers and 153 men were wounded and two officers and 166 men were missing - none of whom were ever recovered. Private Joseph Burgess was one of those originally listed as killed.

Shortly after this, the 2nd Battalion left France for Salonica.

Joseph Burgess is buried at Vermelles British Cemetery, France, in Plot VI, Row D, Grave15 and is also commemorated on the Memorials at Norbury Church and at Stockport Art Gallery.

~~~~~

# TR4/26039 Private Albert **Butterworth**
## B Coy. 63 Training Reserve Battalion
## 21 March 1917

Of all the names on the Hazel Grove Memorial, Albert Butterworth has the unenviable distinction of having served the shortest time in the Army before dying - five weeks. He was 18 years old.

The son of Albert and Fanny A. Butterworth, of 36 Brewers Green, he was born in Hazel Grove and before joining up, worked as a porter at Moseley Street for the London and North Western Railway. A member of the choir at the United Methodist Chapel, he was also connected with their Sunday School.

After being called up, Albert was posted to Kinmel Camp near Abergele, North Wales on 17 February 1917 for his initial training. Shortly afterwards, he suffered a bronchial attack and, despite the attention of a number of doctors at the Military Hospital in Rhyl, this developed into pneumonia. Fortunately a message had been sent to his mother and she was able to be with him when he died on 21 March 1917.

On Saturday 24 March the coffin was brought to Stockport by train and was met by a firing party from Handforth Camp who accompanied the hearse to his parents' home in Brewers Green. London Road was thronged with sympathetic spectators for the journey to Norbury Church for the interment. On arrival at the churchyard, the firing party formed up on both sides of the path and stood, rested on their reversed rifles, with heads bowed. At the close of the commital, three volleys were fired.

The following day, a memorial service was held at the United Methodist Church where, after the war, Albert's name was included on the Memorial. It is now on the combined Memorial in the Methodist Church. Albert is also commemorated on the London & NW Railway Roll of Honour.

Albert Butterworth's gravestone still stands at the far side of the Narthex in Norbury Churchyard, Grave 83. On it are inscribed the words "Thy Will be done". The Stockport Advertiser described him as "A fine lad."

~~~~~

# 36843 Private Frederick George **Clarke**
## "D" Coy. 9th Bn Cheshire Regiment
## 24 March 1918
(Picture)

Codenamed "Operation Michael", the German Spring Offensive of 1918 started on 21 March 1918 with massive artillery bombardments upon the British Army. The 9th Battalion of The Cheshire Regiment was near Bapaume on the old Somme Battlefield when the onslaught rained down upon them and they became involved in the desperate attempts to stop the overwhelming German advance.

Three days later, on the 24th, they were subjected to another heavy barrage which lasted from 9.00am until 10.45am, immediately after which there was a massive German infantry assault. During the intense fighting, the front line trench was lost, but shortly afterwards it was regained as a result of a counter attack.

At 2.00pm, due to the difficulties of their position, the battalion was ordered to withdraw and in the early evening, they held a line to the west of Bapaume. Before they were fully able to consolidate it, however, they were ordered to retire further south to Grevillers.

In seven days, the battalion lost 14 officers and 355 NCOs and men, one of whom was Frederick Clarke who is recorded as having been killed in action on the 24th. Because the battalion was retreating, his grave, if he ever had one, has never been found.

Frederick enlisted on 24 April 1916, and lived with his wife Elizabeth at 6 Grundey Street. He was the son of George and Selena Clarke of London Place, Stockport and was in business as a bootmaker and shoe repairer before joining up. At the time of his death, he was 23 years old.

Having no known grave, Frederick Clarke is commemorated on the Arras Memorial in France. In addition, his name was placed on the Memorial at the Primitive Methodist Church then on London Road, and is now on the combined Memorial in the Methodist Church.

~~~~~~

# Private John Henry **Clarke**
## 2nd Bn. Cheshire Regiment
### 17 May 1939
(Picture)

Jack Clarke's name appears on the Memorial, although he survived the war and did not die until 17 May 1939.

Born on the 6 June 1888, in a house on Hatherlow Lane, he was the son of Edward Thomas Clarke and Sarah Ann Clarke. Edward was a miller and had emigrated from Ireland to Hazel Grove. Shortly after the birth, the family moved to a better house in Grosvenor Street. Jack was baptised at Norbury Church, in a private ceremony, on 13 October 1888 and after leaving school became a hatter at Christy's Hatworks.

After joining The Cheshire Regiment, Jack married Nancy Barratt from Woodford at Cheadle Parish Church in June 1917, and they had five children - Edward, John, Ethel, Kenneth and Leslie. The family lived at 13 Ash Street. His brother Bill, was a blacksmith at the Smithy in School Street.

When the war ended, Jack was demobilised but was unable to find work, so felt forced to re enlist as a regular in his old battalion, the 2nd Battalion of The Cheshire Regiment. In late 1919, this battalion was sent to Turkey as part of the Army of Occupation, where it was stationed in Istanbul.

Hygiene was always a problem for the Army, particularly in a hot country, and Turkish hygiene was worse than many countries. Whilst in Turkey, Jack must have drunk some contaminated water because he caught dysentery and although he survived the infection, he became a carrier and as such, a danger to other people. For the rest of his life, whenever the weather became warm, Jack was confined in various Isolation Hospitals in different parts of the country because the heat brought out the disease, and he had to be kept away from the general population. In the colder weather, he could again come home to his family when he was occasionally able to find work doing odd jobs for a local builder - Andrews Construction Co.

The rest of his life was blighted by the disease as it also affected his general health and on the morning of the 17 May 1939, his daughter Ethel went into his bedroom and found him dead. The official cause of death was pneumonia, brought on by dysentery. He was 51.

On Saturday the 20th May, he was buried at Norbury Church in grave New H87, effectively a victim of the war, for had it not taken place, there would not have been the need for an Army of Occupation in Turkey. The villagers of Hazel Grove certainly thought so - they entered his name on the Memorial. He is also commemorated on the Memorial in Norbury Church.

~~~~

# 17649 Private Ernest **Clough**
## 1st Bn Cheshire Regiment
## 2 September 1918

Killed nearly two years after his brother Frank, Ernest Clough very nearly made it to the end of the war. He volunteered in October 1914, was wounded twice and was killed two months before the war ended. What made it worse for his mother Sarah Clough, was the fact that he was her only remaining son and the husband of her daughter Jessie was a prisoner of war.

After joining up he was posted to France and then, in November 1917, he went with his battalion to Italy , where he stayed until March 1918 , when the battalion was transferred back to France. His final stay there lasted only six months.

Ernest worked at Mirrlees before the war and his father Allen, who was a collier, appears to have died some time between 1910 and 1916. The family lived at 3 Daniel Street, (off the A6, directly opposite the start of Chester Road) in what even in those days was not the best of housing. The foundations of the houses can still be seen near the path at the side of the dentists.

The second time Ernest was wounded was in early August 1917 when he was hospitalised by wounds to the eye and hand. At least these brought about a short respite from the war,for he then had a short leave in early September when he was described as looking "in the pink". Twelve months later, he was dead.

After the German 1918 Spring Offensive had been brought to a halt, the Allies mounted an enormous counter offensive which was unchecked by the Germans, until they were forced to surrender in November 1918. The British had been pushed back many miles, losing the gains made in the horrors of the battles of the Somme and Third Ypres and therefore had to fight their way back through the old battlefields. Although the Allied counter attacks proved to be unstoppable, the Germans did not give in easily, causing many thousands of Allied casualties in the last few months of the war.

On 8 August 1918, the counter offensive was started by the British and on the 21 August, the battalion was marched to Bucquoy to take part in the capture of Beugny - a village strongly held by the Germans who had managed to repulse a previous attack. Being in the northern part of the old Somme battlefield, the ground was terribly battle scarred having been fought over twice. The conditions for the soldiers were therefore extremely difficult.

At 5 am on 2 September, the British barrage started and this brought down a heavy retaliatory barrage on the assembling companies, causing estimated casualties of 50%. Gas and liquid fire were used by the Germans in an effort to quell the attack and shells were falling like hail. Gradually, the Cheshires forced their way into the village where they consolidated and before nightfall, they managed to repulse a strong counter attack. Ernest Clough, however,was one of those who were not to survive the day.

Fortunately, his body was found and he was buried in Vaulx Hill Cemetery, Vaulx-Vraucourt, France, in Plot II, Row C, Grave 2. Before the war he was connected with the Wesleyan Church and Sunday School and is commemorated on the Memorial at the Methodist Church. Interestingly, his name is also on the Memorial at Norbury Church. He was about 31 years old.

~~~~

# 13534 Private Frank **Clough**
## 13th Bn Cheshire Regiment
## 21 October 1916
(Picture)

The Battle of the Somme was drawing to its agonising close when Frank Clough was killed in action on Saturday 21 October 1916 aged 28. He was born in Hazel Grove and the first of Mrs. Sarah Clough's two sons to be killed, but he had given her serious cause for concern before.

In early January 1916 she was informed that he had been wounded when he was struck on the head by a bullet. He wrote home from the base hospital to say that his wound was not a serious one, that she should not trouble about him and that he was making satisfactory progress. She therefore had no need to worry about him. She later found out that the bullet had taken off part of his ear and scarred the side of his head. It was a very lucky escape.On recovery he was granted home leave in May 1916, but soon returned to his unit.

On the day he was killed, Frank's battalion was involved in the last stages of the Battle of the Somme. They were taking part in the Battle of Ancre Heights, where the British were attempting to capture a ridge overlooking part of the Somme battlefield and thus, for one of the few times on the Western Front, overlook the German positions. The ridge ran from just south west of Martinpuich to the high ground north of Thiepval.

Thiepval had been captured and the capture of the ridge would give observation over the Ancre Valley and Grandcourt. Both sides were well aware of its vital strategic importance and the fight was bitter.

On 21 October, the 13th Battalion attacked Regina Trench under a barrage which started at 12.06 pm. The weather had been poor and the ground was a morass.The day was cold (45 F.) and dry and the troops moved forward close under the barrage, finding that the enemy's wire had been cut by the shellfire. They advanced in three waves and took their objectives without too much difficulty. Despite this, casualties were severe, 12 officers and 198 men being lost. Ernest Clough was one of them.

Involved in the same attack were five other battalions in an extended line. Next to the Cheshires was the 8th Battalion of The South Lancashire Regiment, a member of which was William Poacher, also from Hazel Grove. He too was killed and like Ernest, has no known grave.

The news came on the morning of Saturday 11 November 1916, in a letter from the Chaplain of the Regiment, who wrote - "Dear Mrs. Clough - You will have received official notice of the death of your son killed in action on 21 October. I am sorry to say that it is not possible to do more than bury them where they lie when they are killed. In

such cases as this, we know our Heavenly Father receives them into his Kingdom just the same as if they were buried in some peaceful spot at home.
May I offer you my sincere sympathy in your sad loss. May God bless you in your hour of sorrow. "Greater love hath no man than that he lay down his life for his friends.""

It was in fact the first Mrs. Clough had heard of the death of her son and , although certainly kindly meant, the wording left something to be desired. Perhaps this is too critical. With many similar letters to write and little time to do it in, the Chaplain did the best he could.

Frank's grave was never found and, along with 73000 others, his name is on the vast Memorial at Thiepval for men who died in the immediate area and have no known grave. His name is also on the Memorial in Norbury Church and the Memorial in the Methodist Church.

~~~~~

# 265495 Sergeant Stanley **Clough**
## 6th Bn Cheshire Regiment
## 10 January 1918
(Picture)

Born in Hazel Grove and the son of a Hazel Grove man, Stanley Clough has the right to be on the Memorial, but is not.

He lived with his parents, Frank and Elizabeth at 40 Buckingham Street, Bramhall Lane, Stockport. His mother did not come from Hazel Grove, as the Stockport Advertiser described her as a "Stockport Lady", whereas his father was said to be "well known in the village". Stanley was their only son.

Before the war, Frank was a Territorial and a member of the 6th Battalion's Band. He was also a very keen footballer and although he did not live in the village, was a prominent member of Hazel Grove Congregational Church's football team.

Being a Territorial, he was immediately called up and joined the Battalion in August 1914, the first month of the war. The Stockport Advertiser, on announcing his death, stated that he had been wounded twice, but the Stockport Express stated that he had been wounded three times and that as a result, he wore three gold bars on his sleeve.

The Battalion War Diary entry for 10 January 1918 simply states that the battalion was at Ypres and that one "Other Rank" was killed on a cable laying party. That "Other Rank" was Stanley Clough. It was not a lot of recognition for a brave man who had served with the battalion for over four years.

Stanley Clough is buried at St. Julien Dressing Station Cemetery, outside St. Julien, Ypres, Belgium, in Plot I, Row A, Grave 3 and is also commemorated on the Memorial at Stockport Art Gallery. He was 25 years old.

~~~~~

# 12043 Lance Corporal Samuel **Condliffe**
## 19th Bn Manchester Regiment
## 13 February 1916
### (Picture)

The 19th Battalion of The Manchester Regiment was one of the new "Pals" Regiments. When such vast numbers of recruits flocked to join up in 1914, one of the attractions for them was the fact that they could join up with their pals, all in the same regiment. These new battalions consisted virtually totally of new recruits, so went through a longer period of training than other regiments. The result was that they became a much more close knit unit than even an ordinary battalion, which was in any case a very close organisation. The disadvantage of a "Pals" battalion was to become apparent when they first went into battle. The high casualty rate of World War 1 meant that whole communities of young men were wiped out at a stroke.

Samuel Condliffe was born in Sandbach, the son of James and Annie Florence Condliffe of 20, Cooke Street. As a child, he had lived in several places in Cheshire because his father was a police constable who, at the time of the war, was stationed in Hazel Grove. Before coming to the village, he had been in Romiley, where Samuel had attended St. Chad's Church and Sunday School. His connections with Romiley remained because he was employed at Schofield's Bleachworks there. He enlisted in Manchester.

After initial training in England, the 19th Battalion embarked from Southampton aboard S.S.Queen Alexandra on 7 September 1915. For the vast majority, when they landed at Le Havre on the following morning, it was the first time they had seen foreign soil. They were not considered capable of being in the line yet, and so further training in France followed.

On 8 December 1915, they went into the trenches with an experienced battalion in order to learn the ropes and stayed there until 17 December. Further training continued out of the trenches, including forming working parties, and then on 8 January 1916 they went into the trenches on their own for the first time. These were outside Carnoy in France, in what was to become, in six months time, the area in which the Battle of the Somme was fought.

From then until the 7th March, the battalion alternated between those same trenches and billets at Bray-sur-Somme, all the time the enemy being highly active with the use of a good deal of shrapnel. Samuel was killed by the bursting of a shell on 13 February 1916, one of the first casualties of the Battalion. He was 21 years old.

Samuel is buried in Row H, Grave14 at Carnoy Military Cemetery, France. Four months later, on 1 July 1916, his former colleagues attacked the Germans from these very same trenches, and were part of the only British success of that day.

~~~~~

# Arthur **Cooper**

The Commonwealth War Graves Commission, who have details of all servicemen and women of Great Britain and the British Empire who were killed in World War 1, have listed 139 men with either the name Arthur Cooper or simply A.Cooper.

Not one of these can be positively identified as having any connection with Hazel Grove, despite an extensive search and the 1891 Census, which is the latest available to study at the moment, shows no one resident in the village by that name. During the period 1921 (when the CWGC records were compiled) to the end of 1923 (when the Memorial was built), no person of this name died in England or Wales who can be identified as having any connection with Hazel Grove. Regrettably, Arthur Cooper at present remains a mystery.

~~~~~

# 63887 Gunner Edwin **Corbett**
## 111th Siege Battery, Royal Garrison Artillery
## 21 September 1916

" In memoriam of Edwin Corbett, late of Hazel Grove aged 23 who fell in action on September 22, 1916 in France." This entry in the Stockport Express of 20 September 1917 is the only mention in the local newspapers of Edwin's death.

The Commonwealth War Graves Commission give his date of death as 23 September, whereas the Official Records give the date as the 21st.. The Royal Artillery cannot supply any details of their former members because, they say, they were such a large regiment that it has not been possible to keep them. The dates given to the paper and to the CWGC would have come from Edwin's family, so the Official date is the most likely to be correct.

All we can find out about Edwin, is that he was born in Llandysil, Montgomery and that he was the son of Mrs.A. Thomas of 5, Chester Road. Presumably she remarried at some time before the war because Edwin enlisted in Stockport.

Edwin Corbett was killed during the Battle of the Somme and is buried at Dernancourt Community Cemetery Extension, near Albert, France. This is well behind the lines but the Official Records state that he was killed in action. As a member of a Siege Battery, Edwin would have been part of the crew of a very large gun, hence their distance from the actual fighting, but whether he was hit by enemy artillery or there was an accident on his gun whilst it was in action is not known. He is buried in Plot III, Row B, Grave 35.

~~~~~

# 32884 Lance Corporal Arthur **Daniels**
## 8th Bn Cheshire Regiment
## 11 August 1916
(Picture)

The fighting in Mesopotamia (now part of Iraq) was, in its own way, as pointless and wasteful as the Battles of the Somme, Ypres and Gallipoli. The march to the town of Kut, south of Baghdad, was particularly marked by incompetence and needless waste of soldiers' lives. One of those soldiers was Arthur Daniels of 12 Lever Street.

Born in Hazel Grove, the son of Henry and Fanny Daniels, he joined the 8th Battalion and, in July 1915, immediately it had completed its training, the Battalion embarked for Gallipoli. Arthur survived the slaughter there and following the withdrawal from the Peninsula, went to Mesopotamia with his colleagues, arriving on 28 February 1916.

A decision had been made to occupy Mesopotamia in order to protect the oil wells of the Persian Gulf. After bitter fighting this had been achieved but the glittering prize of the city of Baghdad beckoned and, with the agreement of the Indian Government, who supplied most of the troops and equipment, it was decided to press on and take it. Total incompetence reigned. There was no proper organisation of supplies and equipment, the Indian Government appearing to believe that the conquest could be achieved without it. The medical facilities were as non existent as those in the Crimea, 60 years before. The attempt to reach Baghdad failed and the expedition was forced to fall back to Kut-al Amarah where on instructions from the High Command it was to remain until reinforcements arrived. The town became surrounded by the Turks and after a seige of unimaginable horror lasting 147 days (longer than the seige of Ladysmith in the Boer War), it was forced to surrender on 29 April 1916. It was a humiliating occasion and one which had to be remedied.

A force was then sent to recover the position. This time there was a more competent commander with responsibility being transferred to the British. A better organisation was set up and the expedition, including the 8th Battalion Cheshire Regiment, set off to retrieve the situation. It was not, however, as efficient as it should have been.

The expedition was involved in a long march through inhospitable desert, fighting off marauding attacks by the Turks . The intense heat caused immense problems. The troops became worn out by diseases, dysentery, cholera and boils. Vegetables were impossible to obtain and temperatures reached 130 degrees in the tents. Equipment and other supplies were however good, but Arthur did not share in the victories. Somewhere along the way, he contacted dysentery.

He was shipped back to base and then on to hospital in India where he died, aged 20. In addition to the normal terse letter of condolence from the War Office, his parents received a letter from one of Arthur's friends, written the day Arthur died, and informing them that Arthur was very popular amongst his colleagues and that he had passed peacefully away. A Wesleyan Minister officiated at the funeral and representatives of both the Cheshire Regiment and the Worcestershire Regiment assisted. The Union Flag was placed over the coffin as he was laid to rest.

Amongst his possessions when he died were two books, one presented by a Miss Kerrison of Warrington and another with the title "The Happy Warrior", presented by Dr. Waddington. The following inscription was placed upon his grave - "In loving memory of Lance Corporal Arthur Daniels, died August 11, 1916, aged 20 years."

Unfortunately, there was a problem with the ground conditions with the result that many graves were lost, so Arthur's name was inscribed on the Memorial at Kirkee near Poona in India.

~~~~~

# 49550 Private Frank **Daniels**
## "D" Coy. 5th Bn South Wales Borderers
## 30 May 1918

One of the worst situations for relatives was for a serviceman to be listed as "missing". If this happened, there was always the hope that he might be a prisoner, or even so badly injured that he could not be properly identified, but alive nonetheless. For the vast majority of relatives, it turned out to be a forlorn hope. The newspapers after the war contained many advertisements from distraught relatives asking if anyone had seen their son or could give any information about them.

In its edition of 23 January 1919, the Stockport Express contained such an advert, relating to Frank Daniels. His parents must not have been able to bear the suspense of waiting for a response to come through the letterbox for the advert asked for any reply to go to someone else, presumably a relative. It contained a photograph and read - "Any returned P.O.W. able to give any information regarding Private F. Daniels, 49550, 5th South Wales Borderers, D Coy, 16 Platoon, B.E.F., missing since May 30th is requested to please communicate with Mr. George Rowland 15 Ash Terrace, Hazel Grove."

Whether this was successful or not we cannot say, but the family were luckier than most, for Frank's body was later found.

Frank was born on 6 May 1899, at 32 Chester Road. He was the son of Alfred and Alice Daniels, and was baptised at Norbury Church on 11 June 1899. Alfred was a greengrocer whose shop was at 139 London Road (which until recently was occupied by Hazel Grove's main Post Office). At the time of Frank's death, the family lived at 33 Napier Street.

As he was only 19 when he died, it seems, unless he had volunteered under age, that Frank was conscripted. The regiment of which he was a member suggests conscription because, until it was introduced, a volunteer could chose his regiment. It is possible of course that there was a Welsh connection in the family but in the absence of any evidence, it is reasonable to assume that he did not volunteer for The South Wales Borderers.

At the time of his death, the 5th Battalion was acting as the pioneer battalion of the 19th Division and as such, combined the duties of trench digging and mining with bombing and fighting. It was also involved in repairing roads and constructing tramways in close proximity to the enemy trenches.

In March 1918, the battalion was one of those attacked in the German Spring Offensive, and during the rearguard action, they fought as infantry. At 2 pm on 30th May 1918 they were in the line outside Chambrecy near the River Aisne, France, when they were subjected to intense enfilade machine gun fire (ie sweeping from end to end), eventually being forced to retire to a position they had constructed at about 10 am that morning. 12 men were killed, 97 wounded and 19, of whom Pte. Daniels is identified in the War Diary as being one, were missing.

When his body was finally found and identified, Frank was buried in Chambrecy British Cemetery in Plot V, Row C, Grave 7.

~~~~~

# T/294596 Driver James **Daniels**
## 534 Coy. R.A.S.C.
## 28 November 1918

James Daniels survived the war, but only by 17 days. He was 25 years old and died in hospital in Norwich, of wounds received in France.

Born on 22 October 1893, he would appear to have been a sickly child, as his parents, Thomas and Harriet, had him privately baptised at Norbury Church on the same day. He was baptised for a second time, this time publicly, with his sister, on 9 February 1896.

The family lived at 1 Marsland's Yard, which was down an alleyway between 311 and 313, London Road (now The Victorian Oven and Harries optician). It was the only house in the Yard. Thomas was a collier.

Originally, James enlisted in The Lancashire Fusiliers, but he was later transferred into the R.A.S.C. The Stockport Advertiser of 3 August 1917 reported him to be home on leave and stated that he had had "some thrilling adventures".

He was seriously wounded and brought to England for treatment but he died of his wounds on 28 November 1918. His body was brought to Hazel Grove by the London and Northwestern Railway, and he was buried in Norbury Churchyard on Thursday the 5th December, where he was buried in grave 110. This grave was owned by a Mr. Joseph Irwin, of 11 Green Lane. Presumably he was a relative of the family.

The grave no longer exists, but James is commemorated, together with three other servicemen whose graves also no longer exist, on a special stone in the front of the churchyard. He is also commemorated on the Memorial in the Methodist Church.

~~~~~

# 16418 Private James **Daniels**
## 7th Bn Canadian Infantry Brigade (1st British Columbia)
## 10 November 1917

Many young men, driven by a sense of adventure and a desire to "make their fortune", emigrated to the colonies in the years before the war broke out. The threat to the "Mother Country" brought about by the start of the war brought many of them flocking back to join the forces. Others, however, joined the Army of their adopted country and fought alongside the British Army. The Canadians, Australians, New Zealanders, New Foundlanders and South Africans were formidable fighters.

James was the son of Thomas and Elizabeth Daniels of 19 Davenport Road. Thomas was a full time evangelist. James's brother Samuel had enlisted many years earlier and had died of exposure in the Boer War. James himself emigrated to Canada and settled in Vancouver, but on the outbreak of World War 1, he joined the Canadian Army, and returned to England with the first Canadian contingent to arrive. He was wounded at Ypres but recovered and was able to rejoin his regiment.

The regiment fought in the Battle of the Somme and James survived this, but Ypres was not lucky for him, for it was during the Third Battle of Ypres that he was killed. Often known as The Battle of Passchendaele because that village was the objective when the battle commenced on 31 July 1917, it dragged endlessly on through appalling weather, deep mud and unimaginable horror until the 10 November 1917. The casualties are estimated to be about 250,000 killed, wounded and missing on each side and the furthest gain by the Allies was about six miles.

The 7th Battalion was involved in the final and costly attack at Passchendaele, which was captured by the Canadians on the 6th November, but high ground to the north of the village needed to be captured in order that the village could be secure. To call it a village at this point in time is somewhat inaccurate, because by now it had become a total ruin. Hardly a stone was left in its proper place.

The final phase of the battle was launched in pouring rain at 6 am on the 10th November, by the 7th and 8th Battalions. The ground was a quagmire in which those unfortunate enough to be wounded often sank without trace. By 7.30 am both units had captured their first objective, 500 yards away. To secure this, however, the 7th Battalion, which was on the right, had to push on another 300 yards to quell troublesome German machine guns in a nearby trench. When this had been done, the 10th Battalion, which had been in reserve, came forward to continue the battle.

The front was very narrow, made even worse by the failure of the British 1st Division attack on the left. This allowed the enemy to concentrate an unusual amount of artillery against the attacking force and casualties mounted at a startling rate.

That day, the three Canadian battalions lost 1094 men, 420 of whom were killed. The 10th November 1917 is regarded as the last day of the Third Battle of Ypres.

The body of James Daniels was never found and he is commemorated on the Menin Gate in Ypres. He was 28 years of age. His name is also on the Memorial at the Methodist Church.

~~~~~

# 202180 Private Samuel **Daniels**
## 16th Bn Cheshire Regiment
## 19 August 1917

The Primitive Methodist School lost another old scholar when Samuel Daniels died of wounds on 19 August 1917. The Third Battle of Ypres had been raging for two weeks at the time of his death, but even though the 16th Battalion was heavily involved in the battle on that day, Samuel is buried at Villers-Faucon in France, which is a village just north of Peronne. This is at the southern end of the area of the Battle of the Somme, which took place twelve months earlier. Presumably he was wounded when the Battalion was in the area, which must have been some time before, though it is very doubtful that he would have been wounded as long ago as the Battle of the Somme itself.

Samuel was a small man, under 5 feet 4 inches tall, but he was able to join up by enlisting in one of the "Bantam" Regiments. The 16th Cheshires were just such a regiment and were in the 35th Division, which comprised solely of such regiments. He was the son of John and Sarah Daniels of 19 Green Lane and was baptised at Norbury Church on 12 August 1883. John was a carter and Samuel became a hatter working at Christy's Hatworks in Stockport.

Samuel Daniels is buried at Villers-Faucon Communal Cemetery, France in Grave 7 of Row D. He is also commemorated on the Memorial at the Methodist Church and the Memorial at Christy's Hatworks. He was about 34 years old.

~~~~~

# 266596 Private Ernest **Dean**
## 1st Bn Cheshire Regiment
## 14 April 1917
(Picture)

The capture of Vimy Ridge by the Canadians on 9 April 1917 was one of the epic attacks of the First World War. What is not so widely known is that the 1st Battalion of The Cheshire Regiment followed them through the operation. After the attack , they were moved to Carency and were placed on two hours notice in case of a counter attack.

Early on 14 April they were ordered to take over from the 12th Canadian Brigade on the summit of Vimy Ridge, immediately east of Souchez and had to rendezvous by 4 pm. However the Canadians had found out that the Germans had withdrawn, so followed them up.

Eventually the Cheshires found the Canadian front line - established in German trenches at the foot of the Ridge, to the east of Givenchy, just as it was getting dark, but as soon as they were installed, orders were received to fall back, causing considerable confusion. Somewhere in the confusion, Ernest Dean was hit and disappeared, his body never to be found.

Ernest lived with his parents William (a hatter) and Hannah and brother David at 17 Neville Street, though he had been born at 17, Chapel Street. David was also serving in France, but survived the war. Before enlisting in March 1915, Ernest had attended the Wesleyan School and had then become a hatter, but although he had originally enlisted in the Cheshire Regiment, he had not originally been posted to the 1st Battalion. A severe wound which resulted in him being invalided home to England meant that when he was fit enough to return, he was drafted into the 1st Battalion. Ernest was with his new battalion for only three weeks before he was killed. During his time convalescing, he spent periods at several hospitals, including one set up at Heaton Park.

A few days after his parents received the official letter stating that their son had been killed, they received a letter from his platoon sergeant (F.C.Mellor), as follows :-
" Just a few lines on behalf of myself and the platoon to enquire if you have received any information on your son because he is reported "missing" from his company. We all hope you have received news from him and that he is well. He was with us last Saturday going into action but he has not been with us since, so we expect that he went into hospital. While we were in the trenches a parcel arrived for him and we divided it amongst his mates because if it had been returned the contents would have been spoiled by the time it reached England again. I could not find any letters or correspondence but I managed to find your address from one who lived close by your place. He has only been with us for about three weeks and he proved himself to be a good soldier and very willing. I hope you will soon have him home again."

Alas, this proved not to be the case, but there is something puzzling about this. Ernest's body was never found and his platoon sergeant refers to him as being missing. The Stockport Advertiser of 28 May 1917 (only six weeks after he disappeared) clearly states that Ernest had been killed in action, as do the official records.Where a body could not be found, the notification usually stated that a soldier was "missing" Possibly someone came forward later and informed the Authorities that they had actually seen him killed, but that it had not been possible to retrieve his body.

Ernest is one of the 36957 British soldiers commemorated on the Memorial to the Missing at Arras in France, as having been killed in the immediate vicinity but have no known grave, and his name is also on the Memorial at the Methodist Church. He was 29 years old.

~~~~~

# 4434 Private Ernest Horace **Dominick**
## 6th Bn Cheshire Regiment
## 3 August 1916

The War Diary of the 6th Battalion of The Cheshire Regiment for the 3 August 1916, states laconically, " Resting at Le Touret from the Neuve Chappelle/Grivenchy Line. One OR killed by gunshot wounds when on fatigues."

That "Other Rank" was Ernest Dominick and in many ways this terse comment sums up what can be traced about him. There was no newspaper report of his death and the CWGC records give no details of any next of kin or age. He was however, born on 4 September 1892 at 34, Sussex Square, Nottingham, the son of Frank and Sarah Ann Dominick. Frank was a lace maker. The only other information that can be deduced is that he was a member of the Congregational Church, because his name is on their Memorial, which is now in the United Reformed Church in Short Street. Ernest enlisted in Stockport, but whether he moved to Hazel Grove to work, or had moved as a child is not known. There was no family by the name of Dominick in the Hazel Grove Directories of 1907 or 1910 and the 1918 Electoral Roll does not include any person of that name.

Thursday 3 August 1916 was a very hot day. The temperature rose to 84 F. with a clear sky. The Battle of the Somme had started just over a month before with a massive loss of life. From the 23rd of July until the 3rd of September the 6th Battalion was in and out of the trenches in front of Thiepval, rotating with other battalions. On 3rd of August, even though they were resting, they had countless chores to do. If Ernest died of gunshot wounds then presumably he was very close to the front line at the time, possibly carrying stores etc. to the trenches.

Ernest Dominick is buried at Quarry Cemetery, Montauban, France, in Plot II, Row F, Grave 5. He was 23 years old.

~~~~

# 75059 Private Arthur **Eccles**
## 12/13th Bn Northumberland Fusiliers
## 27 September 1918

On 11 August 1918, Arthur Eccles' sister, Mrs. Mary Jane Clough, received notification that he had been wounded in action in France. Presumably it was not a serious wound, because Official records show that he was killed in action on the 27th September following. He must therefore have recovered quickly and returned to his unit. Regrettably it was all too soon before he was killed.

Arthur was born in Poynton, the son of James and Ann Eccles. James was a collier and Arthur was baptised at St. George's Church, Poynton on 30 July 1899, but when he enlisted he was living with his sister and brother in law Samuel, at 20 Brook Street. There is no report of his death in the newspaper. Before he joined up, he was the Hon. Secretary of Norbury Lads AFC, for whom he was also a prominent player, so he would appear to have lived in the village for some time.

By September 1918, the Germans were in full retreat, leading to their eventual defeat on the 11th November 1918. The 12th/13th Battalion, Northumberland Fusiliers was involved in the pursuit, which in their case meant recrossing the old battlefield of the Somme. They were taking constant casualties virtually every day as they moved forward.

At 7.52am on the 27th September, the Battalion attacked the enemy and gained its objectives. In the evening, however, there was a strong counter attack by the Germans and the Battalion was forced to retreat, thus losing the positions gained in the morning.

The War Diary notes that three officers were killed and five officers wounded on the day, but makes no mention of casualties amongst the men. It does note however that during September 43 Other Ranks were killed, 370 wounded and 48 were missing, one of whom proved to be Arthur Eccles.

No trace of Arthur's body was ever found and his name is inscribed on the Memorial to the Missing at Vis-en-Artois (between Arras and Cambrai), France. He is also commemorated on the Memorial at Norbury Church.

~~~~

# 15016 Private Robert Bailey **Fenna**
## 6th Bn Cheshire Regiment
## 13 November 1916

For a number of years, up to at least 1940, the following entry appeared in the Stockport Advertiser edition nearest to the 13th November :- "In Memoriam - In loving memory of Private R.Fenna (Bob), fell in action in France November 13th 1916. Wife and daughter Norah, 30, Chapel Street, Hazel Grove."

Bob was born in Bredbury, but together with his parents, Harry and Sarah Ann, and his sister Nellie, he moved to Hazel Grove sometime before the war. With his wife Dora, he was an active member of the Primitive Methodist Church, and is commemorated on their Memorial which now forms part of the Methodist Church Memorial.

Once again, The Battle of the Somme claimed a victim from Hazel Grove when Bob was killed in action whilst involved in the fighting for the village of St. Pierre Divion to the north of Thiepval, approximately in the middle of the battlefield area. The total length of the British line which attempted to advance was about 18 miles and as a result, over the next five months that the battle lasted, many "sub battles" developed, one of which became known as the Battle of the Ancre. The Ancre was a river running through part of the battlefield.

The 6th Battalion were involved in this battle from the 13th to the 18th November, struggling through atrocious ground conditions of deep glutinous mud. To make movement possible , duck board tracks were laid from Thiepval to the assembly area. The trenches had been so shot about and damaged by the weather that even in daylight it was hard for the Cheshires to locate their position or even say whether they were in their own trench or not. Progress was limited to 15 yards a minute at the most - men had to sit down and pull their legs out of the mud. A slip into a water logged shell hole was almost certain to result in drowning. If it was noticed that a man had fallen in, it was virtually impossible to pull him out, as the would-be rescuers could not get sufficient of a grip to save their colleague. If he were not seen, a man was, on most occasions, unable to grip anything to pull himself out, and slowly sank into the slime and mud.

The 6th Battalion was formed up in a fortification recently captured from the Germans, called 'Schwaben Redoubt' and was ready to attack in four lines as part of the main attack. Zero was fixed for 5.45 am. on the 13th November. The darkness was accentuated by a thick fog which lasted until 9 am and as a result, the Battalion lost direction and at first missed their objective . They were reorganised and later captured it - Mill Trench, which was along the banks of the River Ancre. By noon, all objectives had been taken, including the village of St. Pierre Divion which was riddled with deep tunnels. 130 German prisoners were taken, but there were 167 casualties in the

Battalion. These included Bob Fenna and Frank Middlebrooke, both from Hazel Grove.

At least Bob Fenna's body was found. Frank Middlebrooke's wasn't. Bob was buried in Connaught Cemetery, Thiepval, France, in Plot III, Row L, Grave 6. He was 27. Stanley Powell, who died nearly two years later, is buried in the same cemetery.

~~~~~

# 27931 Private Isaac **Fidler**
## 23rd Bn Northumberland Fusiliers
## 14 July 1917

The Hazel Grove Directory for 1910 shows there to be 12 families with the surname Fidler in the village, but which one Isaac belonged to is not known. In fact, Isaac Fidler is one of the mystery men of the Memorial.

The Commonwealth War Graves Commission, who have the names of all the servicemen and women from Britain, its Dominions and Colonies who died in the war, have only one Isaac Fidler on their records. They have no details of his address or next of kin. The official records for him show him to have been a Private in the 23rd (Tyneside Scottish) Battalion, Northumberland Fusiliers and that he was born in Whitehaven and enlisted in Whitehaven. Normally, if someone enlisted somewhere other than their home town, their place of residence is given, but there is no such entry for Isaac. It could of course be that the records are incorrect on this point. It is also possible that he lived in Hazel Grove as a young man and went back to Whitehaven some time before he enlisted. He is shown as having 'died' on 14 July 1917.

The only civilian of that name who died in the UK between 1914 and 1923, (when the Memorial was built) was an Isaac Fiddler (different spelling) who was 24 years old and was a Steel Furnaceman, living at 39, Pitsmoor Road, Sheffield. He died of an acute kidney infection on 13th July 1917.

If they are not the same person, there is an astonishing coincidence here. Not only did they die only one day apart, but Isaac Fidler of the Northumberland Fusiliers is not shown as having been killed in action, or as having died of wounds, but is simply shown as 'died'. This word was used for servicemen who died as a result of an accident or of illness etc., which is of course, exactly what Isaac Fiddler did.

Are they the same person? There must be the possibility, but how and why he was recorded twice, once quite clearly as a civilian, can only be wondered at. Also, the connection that either of them had with Hazel Grove is not clear.

Against this is the fact that Private Fidler has no known grave and is commemorated on the Memorial to the Missing at Thiepval in France. His battalion was in the area of the Somme at the time of his death, and the Thiepval Memorial is specifically for soldiers who died in the area of the Somme but have no known grave. As previously stated however, he is implied not to have died as a result of enemy action, so he would be expected to have a grave. Perhaps he died as a result of an accident near the front line and so could not be buried, or his grave was subsequently lost. The only possible way of checking to see whether they are the same person would be to try to trace a burial in Sheffield for Isaac Fiddler, but again, the Hazel Grove connection is not clear.

# Gunner William **Fidler**
## "B" Battery, 38 Brigade, Royal Field Artillery
## 13 April 1918

Little information can be traced about William Fidler. He was 23 years old when he was killed in action on the 13th April 1918. This was at the height of the massive German offensive of Spring 1918, when they made one last effort to try to break the Allies. It failed, and led on directly to the Allied offensive which resulted in the defeat of the German Army.

There were a tremendous number of casualties on both sides and William Fidler was one of them. Because the Royal Artillery was such a large regiment, they can no longer supply details of where individual gun crews were at any particular time, so it is not possible to know the circumstances leading up to William's death. We can be fairly sure however, that he would have been involved in the general retreat and attempting to provide artillery cover for this. It would have been a desperate time.

William was the son of Samuel Fidler, a labourer, and the family lived for some time at 154 London Road, ( now part of Bairstow, Eaves,- Estate Agents) but by 1918, they were living at 47 Napier Street. There was no mention of his death in the local newspaper.

The body of William Fidler was never found and therefore he is commemorated on the Memorial Wall of Tyne Cot Cemetrey, outside Ypres. It contains the names of 35,000 men who died in the Ypres Salient after 15 August 1917 and who have no known grave. The Menin Gate contains the names of over 55,000 similar men who died between the start of the war and 15 August 1917, making a total of nearly 90,000 men with no known grave in the Ypres Salient alone.

His name is also on the Memorial at the Methodist Church.

~~~~~

# 5026 Corporal Robert **Gee**
## 81st Ammunition Depot R.A.O.C.
## 19 May 1918

The Commonwealth War Graves Commission have thirteen Robert, or R. Gee's in their records, none of whom have an obvious connection with Hazel Grove.

One of them however, has Stockport connections and presumably he is the one on the Memorial. He was born in Stockport, enlisted into the RAOC in Manchester and was killed in action in France on the 19th May 1918.

Robert was the son of Charles and Frances Gee of Stockport and the husband of Jenny Gee of 47 Menai Road, Shaw Heath, Stockport, but the couple, who had one daughter, may well have lived in Hazel Grove at some time. Before the war, Robert was a blacksmith employed by Faulkners Carriers of Salford.

During the war itself, Robert was awarded a Certificate of Gallantry and Devotion to Duty whilst under shellfire, but his luck didn't last. At a later date he was injured in the leg by a bomb but did not recover from the shock and died in hospital soon afterwards. His Captain wrote -
" He has been laid at rest in a military cemetery, an oak cross being erected with a suitable inscription. His body was followed by all his comrades, myself , and two officers from HQ. Words cannot express the sorrow the loss of your husband has caused here. For myself, I have lost not simply one of my NCO's but a man for whom I had the greatest respect and regarded as a friend. As an NCO he had sterling qualities, and I had for some time recommended him for promotion. His nature and disposition were such as to make him esteemed by all ranks and he will be greatly missed here."

Robert Gee is buried in Ebblinghem Cemetery, France, in Plot II, Row B, Grave 34 and is also commemorated on the Memorial at Stockport Art Gallery. He was 31 years old.

~~~~~

# 28315 Private Herbert **Gleave**
## 11th Bn South Wales Borderers
## 1 September 1917

There was no mention of Herbert Gleave's death in the local newspapers and the available records give little information about him. All that can be found is that he enlisted in Stockport and died of wounds at a Military Hospital just outside Ypres. There were at least six families with his surname in the village in 1910, but the 1891 Census shows David Gleave an agent for the Refuge Assurance Company living with his wife Martha and their children at 44, Commercial Road. The youngest child was Herbert, aged 6. If this is the same person, he would have been about 32 when he died. In 1918, this family was living at 15, Napier Street.

The 11th Battalion of The South Wales Borderers was also called the 2nd Gwent Battalion, presumably because it recruited mainly in that area. How Herbert came to be in it is not known, unless he was conscripted and placed straight into it without any choice. Certainly, he was never in any other regiment.

The battalion was involved in the Third Battle of Ypres (often known as the Battle of Passchendaele) and had taken heavy casualties. On the 2nd August alone, it lost 350 men of all ranks during an attack on the German 3rd Guards Division and during late August it was involved in one of the many vicious small battles that made up the main battle as a whole. This one was called the Battle of Langemarck, after the remains of the village it raged around. The battalion lost just under 100 men in this battle. The village had gained earlier notoriety when, in 1915, it was where the German Army first released gas canisters on Algerian troops and so started the swift escalation to the many deadly gas attacks by both sides during the war.

Many casualty clearing stations were scattered behind the lines and some of them inevitably acquired nicknames. Three big ones, around Proven, a village about 12 kilometres to the west of Ypres, became known facetiously as "Dozinghem", "Bandagehem" and "Mendinghem". It was to "Dozinghem" that Herbert was taken when he was seriously wounded, probably during the Battle of Langemarck.

Herbert Gleave is buried in Dozinghem Military Cemetery, Proven, Belgium, in Plot IV, Row D, Grave 21. Also buried in the same cemetery is Charles Holebrook, who died a week earlier.

~~~~~

# 70699 Private William **Goodwin**
## 58th Bn Machine Gun Corps. (Infantry Section)
## 24 April 1918

Another Hazel Grove resident killed in the German 1918 Spring Offensive was William Goodwin. Born in the village on 17 June 1894, he was the son of John and Mary Jane Goodwin of 293 London Road. John was a coalminer. William became a pupil at the Wesleyan School, although he had been baptised at Norbury Church on 10 March 1901. After leaving school, he too became a miner and was employed by the Poynton Colliery Co before, in April 1915, he enlisted in the 6th Battalion, Cheshire Regiment.

William went to France in September 1916, but during 1917 he transferred into The Machine Gun Corps. Firstly he was placed into 15 Coy. in 15 Division, but later in the year he contracted Trench Foot and returned to Hazel Grove for a spell of sick leave. In December 1917 he was considered fit enough to return to active duty and went this time to 58 Battalion MGC.

It is difficult to trace the whereabouts of members of the Corps. as they were split into small groups and allocated by their Division to various battalions, so his activities on the day he was killed in action cannot be precisely traced. The 58 Battalion MGC was attached to the 58th Division, and on 24 April 1918 they were fighting a rearguard action against the German Spring 1918 Offensive, which had driven a great wedge into the British lines.

Following a heavy bombardment and by using Tanks, the enemy attacked Villers Bretonneux, a few miles East of Amiens and although 58 Division counter-attacked, they were forced to fall back to a line between Hangard Wood and Cachy. Sometime during that day, William was killed and it was not possible to find his body after the war. He is therefore commemorated on the Memorial to the Missing at Poziers in France. His name is also on the Memorial at the Methodist Church. He was 23 years old.

By 1921, William's parents had moved to 275, London Road (now the Ceramica tile shop).

~~~~

# 299 Lance Corporal John **Grady**
## "B" Coy. 2nd Bn King's Own Royal Lancaster Regiment
## 8 May 1915

The curse of Ypres struck the village for the first time when John Grady was killed in action on the 8th May 1915, but on this occasion, it was during the 2nd Battle of Ypres. The later Third Battle caused most local casualties.

The 2nd Battalion KORL Regiment was in the trenches in front of Frezenburg (near Ypres) from the 4th to the 7th of May, but was then relieved by the 3rd Battalion Monmouthshire Regiment and went into reserve. At 7 am on the morning of the 8th of May, the enemy shelled the trenches blowing them in and making them untenable, with the result that when the Germans advanced, they were easily able to capture the British front line. "B" Coy. KORL were therefore sent forward in support, but at 10am, the Germans attacked the support dugouts, inflicting heavy casualties, including the Commanding Officer. The enemy were, however, unable to break into them, but at 11.35 am a message was received ordering "B" Coy to retire towards Potijze, and further casualties were inflicted on the company.

One of those killed during the day was John Grady and his body was never found. He was 27 years old.

By 1921 his wife had remarried and became Mrs. Sarah Frances Hallworth. She was still living at 9, Whitelegge's Buildings in Short Street where she had lived with John. Whitelegge's Buildings were a row of six squalid cottages built in the 18th century, on the site now occupied by the public toilets in front of the Royal Mail building at the top of Commercial Road. The window level was below that of the burial ground of the church across the street and occasionally they were swamped by water running from the burial ground, making them extremely unhygienic. They were condemned as being unfit for human habitation after World War 2, but were not actually demolished until 1958.

John Grady's name is one of the 55,000 names of missing men on the Menin Gate at Ypres.

~~~~~

# 27601 Sergeant Gerald **Griffiths**
## 19 Bn Lancashire Fusiliers
## 31 May 1918
(Picture)

Moses and Hannah Griffiths, of 4 Davenport Road, lost two of their three sons in the war, Gerald being the eldest of the three and the second to die. The knowledge of his death, however, came to them in a roundabout way and for several months they must have had their emotions twisted and turned by the unfolding of events.

Born in Hazel Grove, Gerald was a member of the Wesleyan Chapel and, as he grew up, became a teacher in the Primary Department at the Wesleyan Sunday School. His father, Moses, who was born in Wrexham, was a hatter. His mother had been born in Hazel Grove and the two of them are shown in the 1891 Census, living at 17, Station Street, though at the time they had no children. On the 2nd of July 1915, Gerald went to Salford, specifically to enlist in the Lancashire Fusiliers and after a short period of training, went to France in November 1915.

On the 21st of March 1918, the Germans launched their Spring Offensive and made great inroads into territory occupied by the Allies. The French, who were defending Kemmel Hill, to the South of Ypres, urgently called for reinforcements and as a result, 19 Battalion, Lancashire Fusiliers was rushed up in support.

Between the 22nd and the 24th of April they were engaged in digging a communication trench on the slopes of Mount Kemmel, but at 2.30 pm on the 25th of April the German Artillery opened a heavy bombardment with both high explosives and gas. An infantry assault followed at 6 pm when the Germans overran the French positions and surrounded the Battalion HQ. The Battalion History specifically mentions Orderly Room Sergeant Griffiths and states that he was killed, but it is incorrect. Only one Officer and 17 men escaped. 14 Officers and 333 NCO's and Other Ranks were either killed or missing. Gerald Griffiths' parents were first of all told that he was one of the missing.

Moses and Hannah placed an advertisement in the Stockport Advertiser in June 1918, in a desperate attempt to obtain information about their son and their hopes were raised when, in late July, they received an official notification that he had been taken prisoner and was in a Prisoner of War camp in Germany. No doubt their relief was considerable on receiving this news and it would have been even greater when, four months later, the Armistice was signed. They could now look forward to getting their son back.

Fate was not to be so kind. On the 3rd January 1919, they received a telegram from the Red Cross in Geneva, telling them that Gerald had been taken prisoner on April 25th, but had died of wounds whilst in captivity on 31st May 1918. The blow must have been worsened by the initial information that he was well.

Gerald was 24 years of age and is buried in Tourcoing (Pont Neuvelle) Communal Cemetery, France, in Row AA, Grave 5. His name is also on the Memorial at the Methodist Church. In its report, the Stockport Advertiser remarked that he was a young man who was held in high esteem by all who knew him.

~~~~~

# 25591 Corporal Leonard **Griffiths**
# 6 Bn Seaforth Highlanders
# 23 July 1918

Less than two weeks after they had been told that their son Gerald was not missing, but was a Prisoner of War, Moses and Hannah Griffiths had their elation cruelly shattered. Leonard, their second son, had been in the Army for about two years and had so far remained unscathed, but the news came that he had been killed in action at Epernay, in France. Seven months later they were told that the original information on Gerald had been wrong. He had actually died before Leonard.

Like his brother, Leonard had attended the Wesleyan Sunday School and had become a teacher in the Primary Department. Also the newspaper report of his death stated that he, like his brother, "was held in high esteem by all who knew him". On enlisting he had gone into a Scottish Regiment, The Seaforth Highlanders, but it is not clear whether he volunteered to do this or whether he was drafted in without any choice. Conscription was introduced on 10th February 1916 and Leonard joined up in 1916, but the date is not known. Before that date he could have chosen his regiment. After it, he would have had no choice in the matter. He did, however, go to Chester to enlist.

Not only was his body never found, but even the date he was killed is not known for sure. The official records state that he was killed between 20th and 26th July 1918, but the first newspaper report of his death gave the date as 23 July. During the period 20th - 28th July 1918, the Battalion was involved in attacking the area of Bois de Courton, between Epernay and Rheims, receiving heavy artillery fire from the Germans including gas shelling. At 6am on the 23rd, despite the enemy barrage, they attacked towards their objective, the Bois de L'Aunay, which they eventually reached. The whole situation was very confused and it is clear from the War Diary that precise details of what was going on were not known by HQ. No casualty figures are given for each day.

Leonard is commemorated on the Memorial to the Missing at Soissons, in France, and also on the Memorial in the Methodist Church. He was 20 years old.

Moses and Hannah were left with only one of their three sons alive. He was also in the Army but had served in Ireland.

~~~~

# 27919 Private John **Grundey**
## 9 Bn Cheshire Regiment
## 24 November 1916

Mirrlees provided not only work for the men of the village, but also one of the few opportunities to travel in those times. One person who took advantage of this was Jack Grundey.

He was the son of Joseph (a hatter) and Maria Grundey of 12 Bosden Hall Road and was baptised at Norbury Church on 28th of January 1883. Later, his parents moved to live at 9 Buxton Street. Both Joseph and his son were members of the Conservative Club, Joseph being one of its oldest members. When the opportunity came to travel to the South of England in order to set up a large diesel engine which he had been involved in building, Jack grasped it with both hands and set off to Farnham in Surrey. He must have made a good impression, because he was offered employment in the town and took it, moving his wife and young family to the village of Upper Hale.

The Stockport Advertiser, when reporting his death, states that he "was called to the colours" implying that he was conscripted, but he joined the Cheshire Regiment which, in view of the fact that he was living in Surrey and was in his late 30's suggests that he made the decision to volunteer, rather than being conscripted.

At the end of October 1916, the 9th Battalion of the Cheshire Regiment was involved in the last gasps of the Battle of the Somme. It took part in the fighting for Ancre Heights, high ground around the River Ancre, and the fighting to occupy a German strongpoint called "Stuff Redoubt". The mud was thigh deep and the weather was atrocious, but they succeeded in attaining their objectives. There is no mention of how and when Jack received his wounds, but it is most likely that it was during this fighting.

He was taken from the battlefield and eventually arrived at the 3rd Stationery Hospital near Rouen, where he died at 11.30am on Friday 24th November 1916. His wife Margaret and children were still living in Surrey and their first knowledge of Jack's death was the receipt of a letter from one of his nurses, Sister Ethel, informing her that her husband had died of his wounds. Mrs Grundey then had to tell Jack's parents of their son's death. It didn't help that his mother had been ailing for several months when the terrible news was received. Soon after, Jack's wife decided that she needed to be back home in Hazel Grove, so she and her three fatherless children moved back and tried to make a new life at 1, Spring Gardens. The connection with Mirrlees continued as, on 30 October 1922, Jack's 14 year old son John, started at the Company as an apprentice.

John Grundey is buried at St. Sever Cemetery Extension, Rouen, France, in Block O, Plot II, Row S, Grave 5. He was about 40 years old. Edward Axon, who was killed two years later, is also buried in this cemetery.

~~~~

# M2/227577 Private Frank **Hallam**
## Mechanical Transport Section R.A.S.C.
## 29 April 1918
(Picture)

John Alfred Hallam must have felt that life was treating him well. He had been a fairly humble pattern card maker, living at 227, London Road (now the site of The Village Card Shop) with his wife Emily May, when their only son Frank was born on 29th March 1898. Emily May Clayton, whom Alfred (as he was known) married at Norbury Church on 3 July 1895 lived at 225 London Road and Alfred came from Rusholme. Emily's family owned Clayton's Stores and the young couple set up home next to her parents, between their house and the shop, which covered 229 to233 London Road. The child was baptised at Norbury Church on 12th June 1898. There were also three daughters of the marriage, Elsie (born 8 April 1896), Marjorie (born 5 October 1899) and Muriel (born 19 December 1900). Alfred was, however, an ambitious man, interested in politics and when Hazel Grove and Bramhall Urban District Council was set up on the 30th October 1900 he was elected as one of the first councillors.

As time went by, he climbed the slippery political ladder to become the Leader of the Council from April 1913 to April 1920. He was also elected to be a member of the Board of Guardians of the Stockport Poor Law Union and was a Magistrate. His son Frank was a bright boy, who finished his education at Stockport Grammar School before obtaining employment in the offices of the Hollins Mill Company in Portland Street, Manchester. The Managing Director of this company was Ernest Bagshawe of Poise House, Hazel Grove but whether Frank obtained this job because his father knew Ernest Bagshawe is not known.

Frank was, however, intelligent, well liked and respected, so more than likely fully justified his employment. During his time at Stockport Grammar School, he had learned to play Lacrosse and as he grew up, he became good enough to be a playing member of Stockport Lacrosse Club. The only cloud on the horizon was that at the age of 18, Frank was called up in October 1916 and after undergoing training, left for France in May 1917. For an ambitious man with only one son, this must have been a great worry to Alfred. The one good factor was that although Frank was in the Army, he was at least in a relatively safe job behind the lines. He was in the Army Service Corps., working in the Mechanical Transport Section at "Y" Siege Park, which was situated in the rear areas of Ypres. In February 1918 he came home on a short spell of leave and no doubt reassured his parents how safe it was where he was stationed.

Fate however, decided to take a hand. First the terse telegramme arrived. This simply informed the next of kin that their loved one had been killed. It did express regret, but as it was a standard issue, it didn't actually feel as if any regret was meant. Then three letters arrived in quick succession, one from Frank's officer, one from his sergeant and one from his pal.

The officer, writing on May 1st said, " It is with the greatest regret I have to inform you your son was killed yesterday (sic) in a collision with a train whilst in the performance of his duty. When I heard I immediately went to the scene of the accident; death was practically instantaneous. How sorry I am I can hardly tell you, for he was one of the nicest and best working boys on my column, ever ready to do the work he had set out to do with a willing heart. I have just seen a padre and he will be laid to rest this afternoon in a Military Cemetery. It grieves me very much to write this and on behalf of myself, the N.C.O.'s and the men of the column please accept our deepest sympathy in your bereavement."

The letter from his sergeant said "You will be pleased to know that as sergeant in charge of his section, I have always found him a splendid type of soldier and one who although very young could always be relied upon to carry out whatever duty was placed upon him."

His pal also wrote "Your dear son and I were friends for a long time and I knew his worth, his true kindness of heart and unselfishness. Nothing that one can say in such circumstances can adequately express the feelings which I and all those who knew him entertain for you, but it will be some consolation for you  to remember that your son was held in such high esteem by all of us and we sincerely mourn the loss of a friend who had endeared himself to everyone."

No doubt those letters were read many times by Alfred and Emily, and after the lapse of a considerable time they almost certainly did provide a little consolation, but not much. After the war, Alfred remained on the Council, but was never as prominent as before. He and Emily moved to live at "The Dingle", Chester Road, and it was very much down to his and Ernest Bagshawe's efforts that the fund raising activities which took place in the first three years of the 1920's were successful enough, despite the effects of the Depression, to provide for the cost of the War Memorial gardens. They may have had a vested interest, but those others left bereaved also gained from their efforts.

Frank Hallam is buried at Haringhe (Bandaghem) Military Cemetery, Proven, Belgium, in Plot III, Row D, Grave 20, and is commemorated on the Memorials at Norbury Church and Stockport Grammar School. He celebrated his 20th birthday exactly one month before he was killed.

~~~~~

# 108258 Regt. Sergt. Major James Hammond **Hallworth**
## 3rd Canadian Mounted Rifles Regiment
## 31 August 1943

Born at 250 London Road (now part of the site of Esso Petrol Station) on 28 September 1885, the son of Thomas and Ellen Hallworth, James grew up to be an impressive figure of a man, 6ft. 2 ins tall, weighing nearly 15 stones, with grey eyes and dark brown hair. He had tattoos on both his forearms.

His father was a wheelwright and joiner but James became a plumber when he left school. He was however an adventurous man and decided to seek his fortune abroad, so went to Canada where he settled in Medicine Hat in Alberta. His wife, Mary Sneath Hallworth, did not go with him however, for when he enlisted into the 3rd Canadian Mounted Rifles at Medicine Hat on 30 December 1914, her address was given as 13, Green Lane, Hazel Grove.

Mary continued to live in the village throughout the war, living at 84, London Road in 1915, 47, London Road in 1917 and 293, London Road in 1918 (opposite his parent's house). James arranged that part of his pay should be paid direct to her for the full period of his service.

The 3rd Canadian Mounted Rifles was a brand new unit, and James was made a sergeant on 4 January 1915, five days after he joined up. Training commenced at Medicine Hat until the battalion sailed for England from Montreal on 12 June 1915 on the SS 'Megantic'. James was promoted to Company Sergeant Major on 22 June 1915 and training continued until they embarked for France, landing there on 22 September 1915.

The Canadian Army was reorganised on 2 January 1916 with the result that James was transferred to the 2nd Canadian Mounted Rifles, still as CSM, but whilst on leave in England from 4th to 13th May 1916, he was taken ill with a very nasty attack of Eczema, so was admitted to Chelsea Hospital on the last day of his leave - the 13th, where it was found that he had a tumour in his groin. Attempts were made to cure the Eczema and on 29 June he was sent to Stepping Hill Hospital where on 15 July he had an operation on the tumour. Clearly it was very convenient to be sent to Stepping Hill but his stay there did not last long, for on 25 August he was transferred to Wokingham to convalesce, finally being discharged from hospital on 10 October 1916.

After such an operation he could not return to the Front so was transferred to the Administrative staff at Shoreham. Full fitness still eluded him and on 10 March 1917 he was transferred to The British Columbia Regimental Depot at Seaford where, on 12 October, he fell ill again, this time with severe swelling of his right leg due to water retention. On leaving hospital he was graded B3 as fit for service abroad but not for general service. His doctor stated that it would be at least 12 months before he would recover fully from his latest illness, but he was clearly still efficient because on 7 March 1918 he was promoted to Acting Regimental Sergeant Major.

On 11 November 1918 the war ended but James did not get an early demob. He carried on at the Regimental Depot dealing with all the administration for the Regiment. On 12 September 1919 he was finally sent to the Canadian Discharge Depot which very conveniently was situated in Buxton and, on 12 November 1919, he embarked for Quebec on SS 'Scandinavian'. Landing there on 21 November he was discharged from the Army as 'Medically Unfit for General Service' on 27 November, giving his address as c/o GPO Medicine Hat. His wife was then living at 293, London Road and his total length of service was 4 years 211 days. During that period his hair changed from dark brown to grey.

Mary later went out to Canada and the couple were living at 1003, Ross Street, Medicine Hat when, on 31 August 1943, James died. Presumably his death was related to his war service as his name was later inscribed on the War Memorial in Hazel Grove.

James Hallworth was the last person from Hazel Grove to die as a result of wounds or disease received in the First World War. His name is also on the memorial in Norbury Church.

~~~~

# 154355 Private Joseph **Hallworth**
## 8th Bn South Lancashire Regiment
## 25 May 1916
### (Picture)

Devotion to duty appears to have cost 22 year old Joseph Hallworth his life.

Born at 1, Queens Road on the 9 August 1893, Joseph was the son of David and Dora Hallworth. David was a collier and the child was baptised one year later at Norbury Church, on the 12th August 1894. When he grew up, Joseph followed his father into the pit. On the 12th October 1914, unmarried and living with his parents, Joseph went to Hyde to volunteer and enlisted in the Cheshire Regiment. Some time later, he was transferred into the South Lancashire Regiment.

A few days after Joseph was killed in action, his officer wrote to David and Dora to say- "He was always cheerful, bright and willing, and never shirked any duty, nay more, volunteering for duty when not his turn, to benefit his comrades. I feel his death more also as I am aware that the shot which mortally wounded him was directly meant for myself. We were in a very advanced post.

Private Hallworth was on sentry duty about two yards from where I was sniping. I told him he would be better further away because of the possibility of retaliation. He declined saying that he must be close to his machine gun. I moved to another post. Within five minutes a rifle grenade came over and exploded a yard from him. A fragment just missed his helmet and struck him on the temple. He became unconscious and passed peacefully away on the 25th. His comrades both in the gun section and the platoon are very sorry to lose him. He died gloriously and nobly, right at his post - a true soldier's death. 'Greater love hath no man than this that he lay down his life for his friends.'"

The Stockport Advertiser commented "At the morning service on Sunday the 4th June 1916 at Norbury Church, the vicar Rev. G.N.Wilmer, made a sympathetic reference to the death in France of Pte. Joseph Hallworth of Queens Road and spoke of the ennobling quality of self sacrifice. Fitting reference was also made at the Wesleyan Chapel by the Rev. Mr. Woolsicroft, resident minister. The choir sang the anthem "What are There!" In the course of the service Mr. Harrop rendered "The Trumpeter" on the organ. Hallworth was the first soldier killed who was connected with the school."

Joseph Hallworth is buried at Aubigny Communal Cemetery Extension, France, in Plot I, Row C, Grave 36. He is commemorated on both the Memorial at Norbury Church and at the Methodist Church.

Unveiling of the Hazel Grove War Memorial on the
11th November 1923. The two photographs depict the scenes in the War Memorial
Gardens and in London Road.

Pte. Walter Adshead

Pte. Edward Axon

2nd. Lt. Geoffrey Bagshawe

Frederick Bann

Pte. Joseph Bannister

Sgt. Harry Bowers

Gnr. George Brown MM

Pte. Frederick Clarke

Pte. Jack Clarke

Pte. Frank Clough

Sgt. Stanley Clough

L/Corpl. Samuel Condliffe

L/Corpl. Arthur Daniels

Pte. Ernest Dean

Sgt. Gerald Griffiths

Pte. Frank Hallam

Pte. Joseph Hallworth
[South Lancs. Regiment]

Pte. Joseph Hallworth
[Cheshire Regiment]

Pte. William Hallworth

Pte. Allan Holebrook

Pte. Charles Holebrook

Pte. Reginald Holebrook

L/Sgt. Clifford Holt

L/Corpl. Frank Jackson

Pte. Arnold Jones

Pte. Louis Jones

Pte. Daniel Kilday

Bmdr. John Marsland

Pte. John Martin

L/Corpl. Frank Middlebrooke

Drvr. Jack Ridgway

Rfln. Frederick Rowbotham

Pte. Harold Skeen

Sgt. Gilbert Stanton

Pte. George Stubbs

Pte. George Tallent

Gnr. Winson Tallent

Pte. Frederick Taylor

Capt. Stephen Vickers MC DFC

L/Corpl. Harold Walters

2nd. Lt. Stanley Warburton

Pte. Henry Wood

# 266245 Private Joseph **Hallworth**
## 6th Bn Cheshire Regiment
## 31 July 1917
(Picture)

The first day of the Third Battle of Ypres claimed the life of Joseph Hallworth, but it was to be an agonising wait of a year before his parents were told that there was no hope and that he must be presumed killed. His body was never found.

Born on 13th January 1898 to John and Sarah Hallworth of 20 Hope Street, he was baptised at Norbury Church on 13th March 1898. John was a hatter. Joseph grew up to be a regular attender at The Wesleyan Sunday School where he was well liked by both teachers and scholars. He left school to take up employment with the Hazel Grove Rubber Company.

When reporting that he was missing, the Stockport Advertiser stated that Joseph "was a quiet inoffensive young man and a well known figure in Hazel Grove." He had a sense of adventure though, because he left the Rubber Co. to enlist on December 5th 1914, when he was not quite 17. Presumably he gave the recruiting sergeant a different age. After training, he went to France with the battalion in 1915.

The Third Battle of Ypres was another battle in which the Generals, well behind the lines and living in comfortable chateaux, threw their men at the Germans in well prepared defences during atrocious weather and conditions, and on terrain which totally favoured the defenders. Many of the Germans were protected by massive concrete bunkers which the British artillery could not destroy. The result was another massive bloodbath for the British Army with gains that were minimal.

On the first day of the battle the 6th Battalion, Cheshire Regiment followed the main attack, moving up Pilckem Ridge from Wieltje towards St. Julien, in reserve to their division. The attack started in a terrific downpour of rain, the ground was deep in mud and the men had a difficult time keeping their footing. It was not unknown for a wounded man to fall and be drowned in the mud. During the day, about an inch of rain fell.

The noise of the British barrage on that day was so loud that it was heard in London, but it had not occured to the Generals that one side effect of such a massive barrage would be that it made the ground even more impossible for the infantry.

The battalion managed, despite the conditions, to reach its final objective, known as the Green Line, some 1100 yards north east of St. Julien. It was one of the very few successes of the day. The battalion to the right of the Cheshires was not so successful; it had a very bad time losing many men and was held up short of St. Julien. The result was that a large gap appeared to the Cheshires' right which the Germans exploited, causing many casualties. At the same time, a number of the enemy in front, who had

71

surrendered, took new heart and picked up their rifles. A desperate hand to hand combat ensued.

On top of this, a heavy German barrage and counter attack took place, forcing the line to fall back. The heavy shelling, some of which came from our own guns, continued through the evening causing heavy casualties. During the day, five officers and 193 men were killed or missing with 12 officers and 269 men wounded.

At first, Joseph's parents, who by now had moved next door to 22, Hope Street, were officially informed that he was missing, but then they received a letter to say that he might not be and that they should wait for further information. This finally came at the beginning of August 1918, when they were told that as nothing more had been heard of him, he was presumed to have been killed on the 31st July 1917.

Joseph's body was never found and his name is inscribed on the Menin Gate at Ypres along with 55000 others who died in the Ypres Salient and have no known grave. His name is also on the Memorial at the Methodist Church. He was 19 years old.

~~~~~

# 40358 Private William **Hallworth**
## 2nd Bn South Lancashire Regiment
## 22 March 1918
### (Picture)

William Hallworth, known as 'Biller' for most of his life, was the son of David and Annie Hallworth of Bosden and he was baptised at Norbury Church on the 9th September 1883. David was a collier, but William did not follow his father into the pit; instead he went to work for C. Royle and Sons, manufacturers, of Adswood. He became active in the Wesleyan Church and was a prominent member of the Young Men's Club at the church. After marrying his wife Sarah, they went to live at 13 Bramhall Moor Lane.

Described as ' One who always took life as it came - prepared for anything', he was in many ways suited for service life and enlisted in Stockport on the 1st March 1917. William and Sarah had no children.

As has been explained elsewhere, the Germans were desperate to attack in early 1918 in order to forestall the expected Allied breakthrough, and although the Allies realised that they were preparing an offensive in the Spring of 1918, it was not known where and when the strike would come. On the morning of the 21st March 1918, after a short but violent bombardment and under the cover of a morning mist, the British found out. The Germans had attacked the weak British 5th Army and broke through reasonably easily.

On the eve of the attack the 2nd Battalion, South Lancashire Regiment was in its hut camp in the vicinity of Logeast Wood. At 3 am heavy gun fire was heard in the direction of the front and at about 9.15am orders were received to move forward. Soon the battalion became heavily engaged with the enemy who had broken through the defences of the forward zone and were advancing in dense masses, preceded by detachments of machine gunners.

By 3am on the 22nd the line had been 'adjusted' and the survivors of the battalion had been reinforced by detachments of other units who had become separated from their own units during the fighting of the previous day. As dawn broke, the Germans advanced again and intense trench fighting took place, the enemy being beaten back several times before sheer weight of numbers and an outflanking manoeuvre forced the battalion to fall back.

At about 10am , 40 men were sent out to form a defensive flank near Maricourt Wood and the whole battalion became involved in a desperate struggle to retain its position. Severe fighting continued until about 3pm, by which time, nearly surrounded, they were forced to withdraw.

73

The body of William Hallworth was left behind and was never found. He was 34 years old and his name is on the Memorial to the Missing at Poziers in France. In addition his name is on the Memorial at the Methodist Church.

~~~~~

# 242379 Private Arthur **Henshall**
## 2/6th Bn Lancashire Fusiliers
## 9 October 1917

The Third Battle of Ypres had been dragging on for just over three months. Every time the British decided to attack, it seemed to rain. It almost seemed to the ordinary soldier that the Germans could make it rain whenever they wanted it to and it became part of the folklore of the battle. The combined result of the rain and the incessant shelling was ground that was a complete quagmire and roads that simply failed to exist any more. Still the generals insisted that attacks go ahead.

On the 9th October 1917, well past the time of year considered in the past to be sensible to launch a large scale attack, Sir Douglas Haig, the British commander, insisted that a further attempt be made to capture the remains of the village of Passchendaele. This village had been the objective to be reached within the first few days of the attack which commenced on the 31st July and still it was in German hands. That August had been the wettest in Flanders for 30 years, but still the attacks were ordered, time after time.

On the 9th October, the assault was to be on Poelcapelle, one of the villages on the way to Passchendaele, except that it was no longer a village. It simply didn't exist anymore. Scarcely a stone remained in its original place. It was hardly even a pile of rubble as it had been so effectively bombarded. Nevertheless, it was a landmark on the map and had to be captured.

Seven battalions of the Lancashire Fusiliers were involved in the action, the highest number in any single attack in the war. The two regular battalions - the 1st and 2nd, together with the 3rd/5th, 2nd/6th, 2nd/7th, 2nd/8th and the 19th battalions, were all in one long line in the assault. The weather and shelling had turned the whole area into a sea of mud which came over the knees of the men and where they were in shell holes, the water came up to their waists. Then it started to sleet.

Throughout the night the 2nd/6th battalion struggled to get to the starting line and when they arrived there at 7.30am they were immediately deployed and moved forward, despite the fact that they were exhausted. A further attack was ordered at 4.30pm , commencing with a half-hour artillery barrage, which succeeded in churning up the ground even more and alerting the Germans to the impending attack. They replied with a heavy bombardment which commenced at 5.13pm, and under cover of which they counter attacked. Their attack was beaten off by 5.30pm. The battalion's casualties on the day were 32 killed, 57 missing and 153 wounded

One of the missing was Arthur Henshall. The son of Alfred Henshall, Arthur and his wife Lily lived at 24 London Road. His body was later found and in April 1918 he was declared officially killed in action. By September 1918, Lily had moved to live at 48

75

York Street, Edgeley and by 1921 she had remarried and become Mrs. Worthington, then living at 18, Hyde Road, Woodley.

The day after the Third Battle of Ypres ended, Sir Launcelot Kiggell, Field Marshal Haig's chief of staff, arrived to take his first ever look at the battlefield. After looking around him unbelievingly, he broke down in tears and said "My God! Did we send men to fight in this?" Perhaps that says all that needs to be said.

Arthur Henshall, who was 28 years old when he was killed, is buried at Tyne Cot Cemetery, near Ypres, in Plot I, Row B, Grave 13. Tyne Cot is the largest British War Cemetery in the world and contains 11,500 graves, but Arthur is the only one from Hazel Grove. His name is also on the Memorial at Stockport Art Gallery.

~~~~~

# 54622 Private Harold **Henshall**
# 6th Bn Machine Gun Corps (Infantry)
# 22 March 1918

There was no mention of the death of Harold Henshall in the local newspapers, and very little can be found out about him.

The 22nd of March was the second day of the German Spring Offensive, by which they hoped to break through the Allied lines. It did not succeed, but an enormous number of British soldiers were killed in stopping it. Harold Henshall was one of these. He was 31 years old.

Harold was born in Poynton, but the 1891 Census shows him to be living at 195, London Road, Hazel Grove, with his mother and father, James and Ann Henshall. James was a draper. Some time later, the family moved back to Poynton and when Harold enlisted into the Royal Welch Fusiliers he was still living there. He was not however forgotten when the time came to inscribe the names on the Hazel Grove War Memorial in 1923.

At some time, probably during 1917 when it was formed, Harold transferred into the Machine Gun Corps but we know nothing more about him. Because of the way the MGC was organised, it is very difficult to find out exactly where a small machine gun unit was on a particular day, so it is not possible to give the circumstances of his death. The 6 Battalion MGC was, however, attached to 6 Division which at 7.30am on the morning of 22 March repulsed an attack by the enemy in the vicinity of Vaux and Mericourt Woods, to the north east of Arras. At 9.30am there was a much heavier attack using artillery and trench mortars, forcing the Division backwards despite making numerous counter attacks. By evening there were large gaps in the Division's line, one of the Brigades only having about 100 men left. During the night, the Division was relieved and went into reserve to re-form. During the two days it withstood the German attack, about 3900 of the 5000 men became casualties.

During the 22 March, Harold was killed and because of the retreat and resulting chaos, it was not possible to find his body. He is therefore commemorated on the Memorial to the Missing at Arras in France.

~~~~~

# 202096 Private Allan **Holebrook**
## 1st Bn Cheshire Regiment
## 25 October 1917
### (Picture)

The Holebrooks were a large family, many of the adult males being involved in the building trade as plasterers. The 1910 Hazel Grove Directory shows numbers 1, 3, and 5 School Street being occupied respectively by Allan (Senior) and his sons Albert and Edwin Holebrook, all plasterers, whilst living at 21, Chapel Street, was another son, John Holebrook, also a plasterer. In fact they all worked in the plasterer's business run by Allan Holebrook from his house at 1, School Street. There were also two other sons, Charles and Reginald, who in 1910 still lived with their parents at 1, School Street. They too worked in the family business. A member of the family still lives at that address.

The brothers also tended to have large families. John for instance had ten children, six girls and four boys. Allan (Junior), named after his grandfather, was the second eldest of these and the eldest son, but he did not work in his grandfather's business. He was a goods porter for the London & North Western Railway at Stockport, but had started work in the Post Office after leaving Norbury School . He had attended the Primitive Methodist Sunday School as a boy.

Born on the 6th November 1893 at 325, London Road (where the Cheese Board now is), the son of John and Eliza, Allan was not baptised until the 23 May 1904, when he was ten years old. By then, the family were living at 21, Chapel Street. On the 19th March 1900, the Log Book for Norbury Infants School states that he returned that day from ten weeks absence, but gives no indication of the reason for the absence. His sister, Minnie, remembers him clearly as a jolly, friendly person who was always considerate to others. He regularly helped his mother baking and with the younger children. She also remembers, with total clarity, the day the War Office Telegram came and the great distress of her mother. Only two months earlier, Eliza's brother in law  Charles had been killed, and fifteen months before that, her husband's nephew Harold Walters had been killed on the Somme. Not only was Allan Eliza's eldest son , he was also the chief breadwinner. By then her husband John was suffering from very poor health and young Allan's death would cause the family considerable problems. The grateful War Office awarded Mrs. Holebrook a pension of 8/3d (42p) a week  for Allan's death.

The 1st Battalion, Cheshire Regiment was a regular battalion but its losses had been so devastating that its members now included a very large number of  "Duration only" soldiers. Allan Holebrook was one of these replacements. It was still treated as a regular battalion however and, for the whole of the war, the battalion was never out of the line for any period exceeding one month. The strain on the men must have been almost unbearable.

The spectre of Passchendaele once again cast its shadow on Hazel Grove, for the battalion was moving up to take part in yet another attempt to move nearer to the remains of the village, this time on the left of the attack near the village of Polderhoek, when Allan was killed. Also killed on the same day was Percy Le Vesconte, whose father owned a hairdressers shop in the village before the war. Percy was a member of the same battalion. The attack itself took place the following day.

A few days after the dreadful telegram was received, a letter arrived from 2nd Lieut. E.C.V. Rutter, O.C. 9 Platoon, 1st Bn Cheshire Regiment. Allan's sister still has this letter, written on brown rather thin paper, in pencil in a beautiful copperplate hand -
"Dear Madam,
It is with much regret that I have to inform you of the death of your son 202096 Pte Holebrook A. He hadn't been with us long - but he had already struck me as a very steady and willing fellow in and out of the front line.
It may comfort you a little to know that he was killed instantaneously by a shell with some others of his Lewis gun team, and suffered no pain. You will be informed of the position of his grave (over which a cross was put) later.
Accept my sincerest sympathy and believe me to be yours.
E.C.V.Rutter."

Whether Percy Le Vesconte was one of the team is not known,but he was killed on the same day, and despite Lieutenant Rutter's comments, neither of their graves were ever found, so there is the possibility that this shell killed two men from Hazel Grove.

Allan is therefore commemorated on the Memorial Wall at Tyne Cot Cemetery, near Ypres, along with 35,000 others who died in the Salient between 15th August 1917 and the end of the war on 11th November 1918 and have no known grave. His name is also in the Roll of Honour of the London & NW Railwaymen killed in the Great War and on the Memorial at Norbury Church. He was not quite 24.

Shortly afterwards, the 1st Battalion was sent to Italy.

~~~~~

# 59467 Private Charles **Holebrook**
## 14th Bn Welch Regiment
## 23 August 1917
### (Picture)

Like most of his family, Charles Holebrook worked as a plasterer in the business run by his father Allan from 1, School Street. Having married a few years earlier, he had moved out of the family home and lived with his wife Mary Jane and family at 355 London Road. As well as his nephew young Allan in the Army, he had one brother (Reginald) undergoing training and another who had been in the Army but was now working on munitions. His father, Allan (Senior), had been a sergeant in the 5th Cheshire Volunteers when he was younger, though by 1917 he was 75 years old.

Born on the 6th February 1879, the son of Allan and Anne Holebrook, Charles had attended Norbury School and on 22nd February 1892 he, together with Ernest Marriott (who also died in the war), took and passed their Labour Certificate Examination in Stockport. He was therefore able to leave school and become an apprentice to his father. As well as attending Norbury School, he had attended the Sunday School and was a regular attender at the church.

Originally he went into the Cheshire Regiment but was later transferred into the Welch Regiment ( the unusual spelling is correct). In official records, the actions which took place on the 22nd August 1917 are described as "minor". Even so, they cost Charles Holebrook his life. The 14th (Swansea) Service Battalion of the Welch Regiment formed part of the 38th Welsh Division and they were in the front line to the East of Langemarck, outside Ypres. Their task was to move towards Poelcapelle and for once they were not given an objective which was totally beyond the bounds of possibility. It was a warm day, the temperature reaching 78F with heavy cloud cover. Charles was severely wounded during the day and was evacuated to a Military Hospital to the rear of Ypres where he died the following day.

Charles Holebrook, the brother of Reginald Holebrook and the uncle of Allan Holebrook (junior) and Harold Walters, all of whom were killed in the war, is buried at Dozinghem Military Cemetery, Belgium, in Plot III, Row H, Grave 2 and is also commemorated on the Memorial at Norbury Church. He was 38 years old. Also buried in the same cemetery is Herbert Gleave, who died one week later.

~~~~~

# 201603 Private Reginald **Holebrook**
## 4th Bn Cheshire Regiment
## 25 October 1918
### (Picture)

Exactly one year to the day after his nephew Allan died, "Rigg" Holebrook as he was known, was also killed. He was 37. Only 14 months had passed since his brother Charles had been killed. He was the last of the four members of the family to die in the war.

Born on the 26th March 1881 at 1, School Street, where he lived all his life, he was the son of Allan (Senior) and Anne Holebrook and worked in his father's plasterer's business. He never married and is remembered by his niece as someone who was always prepared to play with the younger members of the family. He is also remembered in the family for his somewhat "devil may care " attitude which often got him into trouble. The Log Book of Norbury Upper School confirms this by an entry on the 26th April 1894 - " Punished Reginald Holebrook (Half timer) Standard 5, for gross misconduct - throwing the contents of an inkwell onto a girl's pinafore and also for using impudence to a teacher".

The Army was able to use some of his energies and by October 1918, he and his colleagues had withstood the German Spring 1918 onslaught and had fought the enemy to a standstill. Then the Allies struck back, fighting their way back over the previous battlefields and on to new ones. The Germans, though by now exhausted and heading for ultimate defeat, didn't give up easily. They pursued a "scorched earth" policy and booby trapped everything they could. Allied progress was therefore both slow and dangerous.

On the 25th October 1918, the 4th Battalion were in the area South of Courtrai in Belgium and were involved in an attack just east of the Courtrai to Bossuyt Canal. They cleared the whole front of the canal from Knokke (south east of Courtrai) southwards and gained their final objectives on the River Scheldt by dusk that evening. During the whole of October, the battalion lost 14 officers and 297 men, one of the latter being Reginald Holebrook, the official records stating that he was killed in action on the 25th October.

By a strange coincidence, one of Reginald's nephews served in exactly the same area during World War 2.

Reginald Holebrook is buried in Harlebeke New British Cemetery, Belgium, in Plot V, Row C, Grave 11. His name is also on the Memorials at Norbury Church and the Primitive Methodist section at the Methodist Church.

~~~~~~~

# 33387 Lance Sergeant Clifford Holt
## 2nd Bn Cheshire Regiment
## 10 October 1918
### (Picture)

Clifford Holt was a strong young man who was probably a good cricketer. He was a bomber in his battalion and these men were specially selected for their ability not only to carry a large number of Mills Bombs, but also to be able to throw them some distance and with some considerable accuracy.

Before he enlisted in January 1916, he lived with his parents George and Elizabeth Holt at Green Mount, Dialstone Lane, and had attended the Commercial School in Stockport where, during his last year there, he became Head Boy. After leaving to start work, he eventually became Works Manager at the Stockport Rubber and Vulcanite Co. Ltd, Newbridge Lane, despite only being 24 years old and having worked there for only five years . Also, in his less than three years in the Army he had been promoted to the rank of Sergeant, so he must have been a young man with both drive and determination. He was a regular churchgoer at the Wesleyan Sunday School and Chapel.

British and French troops were sent to Salonika (Greece) to support the Serbs against Bulgaria and Turkey both of which had joined the war on the German side. The 2nd Battalion, Cheshire Regiment arrived there in November 1915, immediately after they had been heavily engaged in the Battle of Loos (between Lille and Arras in Northern France). Clifford joined them in October 1916, after he had completed his training.

In September 1918, the 2nd Battalion was near Lake Doiran in Northern Greece, where there had been a stalemate for nearly two years. To break this, it was decided that an attack should take place on 'Pip Ridge', said to be 'The strongest natural fortress in Europe.' This attack, which took place after a preliminary bombardment lasting four days, started on the 15th September and it was on the 18th September that Clifford was seriously wounded. The attack was made by the Cretan Brigade who were followed through by the Cheshires. The Cretans managed to force their way through the Bulgars, but a considerable amount of skimishing went on as the Cheshires came through with the result that Clifford sustained very severe wounds.

On the 7th October, his parents received the news that he had been dangerously wounded and was in hospital in Salonika, and about two weeks later they were told that he had died of his wounds on the 10th October.

Clifford Holt is buried in Grave 599, Mikra British Cemetery, Kalamaria, Greece, the same cemetery as Ernest Howe who had been a doctor in Hazel Grove before he had also joined up. Clifford is also commemorated on the Memorial at the Methodist Church.

~~~~~

# 92188 Gunner Herbert **Hooley**
## 95th Siege Battery, Royal Garrison Artillery
## 3 August 1917

The rain poured down on Tuesday the 31st July 1917, the first day of the Third Battle of Ypres, and it was still pouring down on Friday the 3rd August, when Herbert Hooley was killed in action.

The Royal Artillery cannot now say precisely where his battery was on that day, but as he was part of a Siege Battery, he would be working a big gun and therefore some distance behind the lines. If he was buried reasonably near where he was killed, then his battery was behind the town of Ypres. The problem they mainly had was to keep firing when every time they did so, the gun sank further into the mud. The water cascaded from the sky and turned every trench into a stream and every stream into a torrent. The water had nowhere to run. Just below the surface of the Flanders Plain was solid clay so when the topsoil was saturated, water simply stayed on the surface. If the guns could be fired, getting ammunition to them became well nigh impossible. Shells stored by the guns sank out of sight into the mud and those that didn't had to be thoroughly cleaned before being loaded, slowing down the firing.

On top of this, the Germans were not sitting idly by whilst they were being attacked. They were on the high ground, in concrete bunkers. Not only could they see everything the British were doing but they were protected from the rain and shelling by their fortified emplacements. Machine guns sought out the attacking British Infantry and mowed them down like corn. Heavy German artillery sought out the British guns who, like the infantry, had little by way of protection. The British High Command considered that to provide this showed a 'defensive mentality' and was not therefore to be encouraged. Presumably Harry, as he was known, was caught by one of these searching guns.

Such was the chaos of those first few days of the battle that it was not until the end of August that his wife Jane and young child, living at 312, London Road, (now part of the Nobin Restaurant), received the news of his death. Herbert, the son of George and Mary Hooley of 26, Heathland Terrace, Shaw Heath, had married Jane Maria Tomlinson of 10, Marsland Street, Hazel Grove at Norbury Church on 10 May 1911. Herbert gave his age as 24 and was a painter. They had one son, Colin, born on 23 March 1913.

Herbert Hooley is buried at Vlamertinghe New British Cemetery, Belgium, in Plot V, Row B, grave 36. The CWGC records show him to have been 32 years old and his name is also on the Memorial at Norbury Church. The Stockport Advertiser described him as 'a genial young man.'

# Lieutenant Ernest **Howe** MB, ChB
## 38 Field Ambulance R.A.M.C.
## 14 December 1916

For a number of years, Hazel Grove had only two doctors, Dr. Moore and Dr. Tomlinson. Dr. Moore was then joined in his practice at Moseley House, London Road, (where the clinic now stands) by his son. Dr. Tomlinson, who practised at 18/20, Davenport Road, then took on Ernest Howe as a junior partner in 1911.

Ernest was born in Dove Holes in about 1886 and was the son of John and Anne Howe. John had been a preacher in the Hazel Grove Primitive Methodist Church since some time in the middle 1880's and Ernest and his mother also worshipped there.

After graduating from Manchester University in 1909, Ernest obtained a post at Manchester Royal Infirmary, where he stayed until moving to Hazel Grove. He joined the Army in 1916 and left Southampton for Salonika at the end of October of that year. Just over a month later, he was dead.

On arrival in Salonika, Ernest was sent to 83 Field Ambulance, who were in a tented encampment at Tasli in Northern Greece. On the 14th December, the camp was attacked by a single German plane, which dropped one bomb. That bomb killed the Chaplain, one member of staff and one patient. Ernest Howe was severely wounded and died shortly afterwards. They were all buried at the camp the following day, but after the war they were reburied at Mikra British Cemetry, Salonika. Ernest was buried in Grave 1884. He was 30 years old.

By 1918, his wife Gertrude and his two young children had gone to live at 'Croyde', Mauldeth Road, Rhos on Sea, Denbighshire.

Ernest's name is also on the Memorial at the Methodist Church.

~~~~~

# 54252 Private Reginald **Hunt**
## 12th Bn Manchester Regiment
## 13 September 1918

Reginald Hunt was the second Hazel Grove policeman's son to be killed in the war, the first being Samuel Condliffe. Both of them were in the Manchester Regiment, though in different battalions. He was the youngest of five soldier sons of John and Martha Hunt of 361 London Road and was 22 when he died. His brothers were Thomas, a sapper in the Royal Engineers, who had been reported killed before Reginald, but eventually this was found to be incorrect; Joseph, who had been transferred out of the Army to undertake munitions work; Jack, a driver in the R.A.S.C. in France, and Jim, who was in the Royal Naval Division and at the time of Reginald's death was in England recovering from Trench Foot.

Originally, Reginald had enlisted in the Duke of Lancaster's Own Yeomanry, but when this, like many of the Yeomanry Regiments was disbanded, he had been transferred into the Manchester Regiment.

On the 10th September 1918, at 1.00am., the battalion moved up to an attack position, where they could overlook the railway line, Gauch Wood and Villers-Guislaine on the Hindenburg Line, to which the Germans had retreated after their defeats in the August battles. At 5.30am without any preliminary bombardment, the 12th Battalion started its attack, under cover of a heavy barrage, which started as soon as they moved off. The idea was to give the Germans no warning, but to pin them down as the attackers left their trenches.

Two of the battalion's companies reached their objectives easily but a third took heavy losses. The Germans began their counter attack as soon as dawn broke and the Manchesters were not helped when German prisoners attacked them at the same time. This developed into fierce hand to hand fighting, again resulting in heavy losses by the Manchesters.

By about 1pm, things had started to settle down when movement was seen some distance away. On investigation the battalion captured 44 Germans.

Another German counter attack started at dusk with an artillery bombardment of the Manchester positions which continued until daybreak on the 11th. The battalion was then involved in heavy fighting for the rest of the day, receiving very heavy losses. That night the battalion was relieved and went into reserve.

Reginald Hunt died of wounds on the 13th September, so probably received them during this fighting. He was buried at Abbeville Communal Cemetery Extension, France, in Plot IV, Row E, Grave 25 and is commemorated on the Memorial at Norbury Church.

~~~~~

# 8679 Lance Corporal Frank Andrew **Jackson**
## 17th Bn Manchester Regiment
## 1 July 1916
### (Picture)

Saturday 1st July 1916 has gone down in British history as the worst disaster ever to befall the British Army. On that one day, in one battle, nearly 60,000 men became casualties. How many of them came from Hazel Grove cannot be known, but only one man from Hazel Grove died. He was Frank Jackson of 4 Holly Bank, Davenport Road (now the small car park on the corner of Hatherlow Lane and Davenport Road).

Ralph Linton Jackson, a joiner, and his wife Sarah Ann Jackson, were living at 1 Napier Street, when their son Frank was born on the 14th June 1891. He was baptised at Norbury Church on the 26 August 1894, and as he grew up, Frank developed a skill in reciting, so much so that he soon came in demand to recite at entertainments in the area and achieved a small amount of local fame. After leaving school, he went to work at the firm of Blair and company, carpet manufacturers, Manchester, and one day whilst in Manchester, he walked into the local recruitment centre with some of his colleagues and joined the 2nd Manchester Pals Battalion (17th Manchesters).

After completing their training, the 17th Battalion embarked for France from Folkestone on the 8th November 1915 and arrived in Boulogne. Further training continued and they went into the trenches for the first time on the 9th December, where they carried on their training as they were destined for bigger things.

If the German High Command could have chosen a place that they wanted the British to attack, it would have been in the area of the River Somme. They had been able to strongly fortify their positions there and had sited them on high ground which would give them a commanding view over any British attack. They couldn't believe their luck when, because of the amount of activity in the area, they realised that this was precisely where the British had decided to carry out their major campaign in 1916.

The British artillery barrage started five days before the infantry attack was due to start, the purpose being to destroy the German barbed wire and defences. Despite being one of the biggest barrage in history at that time, if not the biggest, it failed. In most places it simply did not destroy the wire and the German troops were deep underground in their dry, comfortable concrete bunkers. Unlike Belgium, here the land was dry and the rock chalk. When the barrage stopped, they came quickly to the surface to be amazed to see the British troops walking steadily across No Man's Land. Some were even kicking footballs as they advanced, having been told by their commanders that no Germans could possibly survive the bombardment. German machine guns simply wiped them out. Very few even got as far as the barbed wire, let alone through it.

The men of the 17th Battalion were not of course aware of what awaited them as they moved up to their starting line on the 30th June. They crowded into the trenches where they found it impossible even to sit down as there were so many of them. The night was cold and morning broke with a chill white mist on the ground. Just before zero hour of 7.00am, the British barrage rose to a crescendo and then the first wave, (19th Manchesters) rose at exactly 7.00am to start their advance.

The 17th Battalion were to form part of the second wave and left the trenches at 8.30am and set off to cross the exposed two miles to their objective. It immediately became clear that things had not gone as planned. On their left, the 18th Division had been held up by a strong point named Pommiers Redoubt, with the result that as the 17th Battalion tried to get past, they were enfiladed by rifle and machine gun fire, causing many casualties.

Although the actual German front line trenches had been badly damaged by the British artillery, the battalion's casualties were very high and "A" Company was wiped out. In their eagerness to get on with the attack, the battalion advanced too quickly and caught up with their own barrage, so had to lie down for 40 minutes before they could rush forward to capture the village of Montauban. This they did at 10.05am but were still being enfiladed from the left. They then continued their attack northwards, coming under increasing shellfire. Eventually they reached their objective but, because of the enemy barrage raining down on them, they were unable to dig new trenches, causing them even higher casualties. Almost half the battalion strength were wounded or killed. During the day, the sun shone brightly and the sky was clear. The temperature reached 72F, with the result that many wounded men lying in shell holes or wherever they could find shelter suffered from the sun as well as their wounds.

The 30th Division, of which the 17th Manchesters were a part, was the only Division on the Somme to reach its objectives on that day, but Frank Jackson was one of the day's 60,000 casualties. His body was never found, and his name is one of the 73000 names on the Thiepval Memorial to the men who died on the Somme between 1st July 1916 and 20th March 1918 and have no known grave. His name is also on the Memorial at Norbury Church. He was 25 years old.

Among the many letters of condolence received by Mr. and Mrs. Jackson was one from Frank's former employer Mr. Blair, in which he wrote - "He was a fine young fellow and I am sad to think he is gone. He was one of the nicest young men and I assure you I shall miss him very much. I hope you will be able to bear the thought of his loss."

~~~~~

# 18562 Lance Corporal Charles **Johnson**
## 9th Bn Cheshire Regiment
## 31 May 1918

There was no mention in the local newspapers of the death of Charles Johnson, his body was never found and the Commonwealth War Graves Commission records give no details of any next of kin.

Official records show, however, that he was born in Hazel Grove and enlisted in the Cheshire Regiment in Stockport, but nothing else can be found out about him.

Because of the date of his death, we can say that he was involved in the hasty retreat brought about by the German Spring Offensive of 1918. The 9th Battalion had been retreating continuously since the start of this offensive on the 21st of March and was therefore withdrawn towards the end of May to rest and reform.

It was not to be, because on the 27th May the Germans made an unexpected attack in a different area - the Chemin des Dames - after what was later reckoned to be one of the heaviest barrages of the war, and overran the front line. The 9th Battalion was therefore hastily moved from the rest area to the fighting at Chaumuzy on the 28th and at about 5.00pm on the 30th, they repulsed an attack by using machine guns and rifle fire. At the time they were holding a good position on high ground to the north of Sarcy, but that evening were ordered to withdraw to the south of Sarcy.

At midday on the 31st May the Germans attacked them again, with an artillery barrage and machine gun fire. This time, the Germans were on the high ground and by mid afternoon, the Cheshires' line was an inferno of high explosive and machine gun fire, forcing them to withdraw at 3.15pm. Later in the day, they carried out a successful counter attack. Charles Johnson was one of the 97 casualties.

In addition to being commemorated on the Memorials at both Norbury Church and the Methodist Church, Charles' name is on the Memorial to the Missing at Soissons, France.

~~~~~

# 100685 Private Frank **Johnson**
## 2nd Bn. Kings Own Royal Lancaster Regiment
## 19 September 1925

For some, the war didn't just injure them physically, it injured them mentally too and their suffering carried on after the war ended. In the dead of night for many years after the war ended, it was a common sight in the villages and towns of Britain to see men tramping the streets. They were unable to sleep because of the nightmares that haunted them and their only relief was to walk away the nights, where they regularly met others in a similar plight.

One such man was Frank Johnson of 7, Ash Street. He was born in Hazel Grove and as a child and young adult he had been a regular attender at the Wesleyan Church and Sunday School. When, in December 1915, that church published its 'Roll of Honour' listing all the men of the Church and School who were serving in the Armed Forces, Frank was listed as being a prisoner of war.

It is not now possible to find out when he was taken prisoner, but he was not released until after the war ended and it very soon became clear when he arrived home that he was mentally ill. The cause is not known. It could have been shellshock, the result of prolonged imprisonment or something which would have happened anyway, but the result was the same. Frank was not the man he once had been.

Eventually it became clear that he could no longer remain at home. The effect on his two young children, his wife Annie and his mother Mary must have been devastating. The Military Authorities decided that the only thing to do was to take him into hospital to see what could be done for him, and he was therefore taken to the Lancashire County Mental Hospital at Rainhill, near St. Helens, where he stayed until he died on Saturday the 19th September 1925 aged 33. The cause of death given on his death Certificate is acute Osteo Myelitis which is inflammation of the spinal column. Whether this was a polite way of describing his mental illness or whether his death had no connection with his mental health can no longer be found out. By then, the family were living at 15, London Road.

On Wednesday the 23rd September 1925, after a service at the Wesleyan Church, his coffin was covered with the Union Flag and was transported to Norbury Church where it was buried in grave New F 98. Members of the 60th (6th Cheshire and Shropshire) Medium Brigade, Royal Garrison Artillery, acted as bearers and walked alongside and the hearse was followed by five coaches containing the mourners.

By then, the War Memorial had been erected, but Frank's name was later inscribed upon it, a recognition by the people of the village that Frank Johnson was just as much a victim of the war as a man who had died in the trenches. His name is also on the Memorial in the Methodist Church.

# 4397 Private Leonard **Johnson**
## 6th Bn Cheshire Regiment
## 28 August 1916

For some men, their time in the trenches was dramatically short. One such man was Leonard Johnson who was only in France for about six weeks when he died of wounds on the 28th August 1916. Leonard enlisted into the Cheshire Regiment, but was attached to the 5th Battalion, Kings Own Royal Lancaster Regiment when he died. The reason for this is not known, but the Battle of the Somme started less than three weeks after he arrived in France, so possibly he was attached to that battalion to make up for the men lost. As he died of wounds, it is not known exactly when he was wounded, but in view of the date it is a reasonable assumption that it was during the Battle of the Somme.

Leonard Johnson enlisted on the 18th October 1915 in Stockport. He was a single man of 35 who lived with his parents, Joseph and Jane, in Fence Street. Prior to enlisting, he had worked for 20 years for Christy's Hatworks without having taken a single day off sick and was noted at work for his great punctuality. On 10th July 1916, just after the start of the Battle of the Somme, he left England to join his battalion, but at the end of August, his parents received notification that he was in hospital, seriously wounded in the shoulder and lung and was very ill. The matron wrote to his parents saying that Leonard "was a very good patient and that it is hoped that he might soon feel better". It was not to be. Soon after, another letter arrived stating that on being visited one evening and being asked if the gramophone disturbed him, he replied that he was enjoying it. In the night however, he was taken worse and passed quietly away on August 28th.

At the morning service at Norbury Church on 3rd September, the vicar announced a special hymn to be sung in Leonard's memory and at the Congregational Church where some members of the family worshipped, Mr Jackson, the organist, played ' O rest in the Lord', "the congregation reverently standing".

Leonard Johnson was buried at Abbeville Cemetery, France in Plot III, Row D, Grave 20. He is commemorated on the Memorials at Norbury Church and at Christy's Hatworks.

~~~~~~

# 26389 Private Arnold **Jones**
## 7th Bn Kings Shropshire Light Infantry
## 21 August 1918
(Picture)

To have one son killed in action must have been a dreadful experience for any parent and to have two killed, as happened to several parents in Hazel Grove, must have been devastating. To have two sons killed the day after each other even though they were in different regiments and different parts of the Western Front must have been beyond belief. It happened to John and Emily Jones of 115 Commercial Road .

There were three brothers, Louis the eldest, Arnold and Norman, all of whom were in the Army and all of whom had previously worked at Bredbury Colliery. They had all been born when the family lived in Offerton before moving to Hazel Grove and were connected with the Primitive Methodist Chapel and School in Hazel Grove before joining up. Louis was married and lived elsewhere in the village, but Arnold and Norman still lived at home when they enlisted.

Arnold volunteered for the Cheshire Regiment in 1914 at the age of 18 and at a later date was transferred into the KSLI. After training in Oswestry, he went out to France in September 1916 and in the following twelve months he was twice wounded and once in hospital with 'fever'. In November 1917, he came home on leave and had only been back a short time when he had a serious attack of 'fever' again. His last letter home, saying that he was fit and well and that he expected to be home on leave again shortly, arrived on the day he was actually killed.

On the 21st August 1918, the 7th Battalion KSLI was involved in the Second Battle of Albert, where part of the battle of the Somme had taken place two years earlier. Having soaked up the German Spring 1918 Offensive, the Allies counter attacked and pushed the enemy back until the Germans surrendered on the 11th November 1918. The battalion was one of the two leading battalions of the 8th Brigade.

Their objective on the 21st August was the railway line between Bapaume and Arras and they commenced their attack at 4.55am, reaching the railway at 7.30am. The Germans resisted strongly with the result that the final assault had to be made with the bayonet. There were heavy losses on both sides. During the period 19th to 24th August, the battalion had 242 casualties, one of whom was Arnold Jones.

Arnold has no known grave and is therefore commemorated on the Memorial to the Missing at Vis-en-Artois, France, as well as on the Memorials at Norbury Church and the Methodist Church (Primitive Methodist section). He was 22 years of age. A memorial service for both brothers took place at St. John's Church, Offerton on 22nd September 1918. By 1921, when the CWGC records were compiled, his mother had become a widow and was living at 6, Brooks Avenue.

~~~~~~

91

# 204694 Private Louis Brereton **Jones**
## 23rd Bn Middlesex Regiment
## 22 August 1918
(Picture)

Louis was the eldest of the three Jones brothers and unlike the younger two, he was married. He lived at 10 Grundey Street with his wife Mary. A keen footballer, he was well known in the village for his prowess at the game. The 23rd Battalion, Middlesex Regiment was nicknamed ' The 2nd Football Battalion' and it therefore seems likely that when he volunteered in February 1917, he specifically asked to join this regiment.

Like his brothers, Louis was born in Offerton and worked at Bredbury Colliery, where it would seem that he might well have been a safety officer of some kind because he was qualified in First Aid and was a member of the St. John's Ambulance Brigade. The Army made use of this skill and made him a stretcher bearer.

On joining the Middlesex Regiment, he went to Canterbury from where, after a short period of training, he went to France. In November 1917, his battalion was sent to Italy and the local newspaper reported that whilst there 'he had some exciting experiences'. The battalion was urgently sent back to France in March 1918 in order to help resist the massive German offensive which started on the 21st of that month.

By the end of August 1918, the battalion was fighting at Kemmel Hill, south of Ypres in Belgium. This hill is about 350 feet high and, in the flat terrain of Flanders, is the highest 'peak' in the province. As such, it was a vital strategic point for both sides and the fighting was therefore particularly fierce. There, on the 22nd August, the day after his brother had been killed near the Somme in France, Louis was killed whilst acting as a stretcher bearer.

His wife received the news three weeks later, just a day or so after the news of his brother's death. The feelings of their parents are difficult to imagine. They were now left with only one son, Norman, who at the time, was in training in Whitstable, Kent. He survived the war.

The joint memorial service took place at St. John's Church, Offerton on the 22nd September 1918, and like his brother, Louis has no known grave. Mr and Mrs Jones must have wondered what more could befall them but within three years, Mr Jones too was dead.

In addition to being commemorated on the Memorial at Norbury Church and the Primitive Methodist section of the Memorial at the United Reformed Church, Louis' name is on the Memorial Wall at Tyne Cot Cemetery, near Ypres in Belgium. Louis Brereton Jones was 25 years old and had married Mary Beswick, aged 22, at Norbury Church on 16 April 1917. They were married for just 16 months.

~~~~~

# 46928 Private Daniel **Kilday**
## 19th Bn Kings Liverpool Regiment
## 28 March 1918
### (Picture)

Daniel Kilday was another victim of the German Spring 1918 Offensive. He was born on 10 December 1882 at 27, Duke Street, Stockport, the son of James (a cotton spinner) and Frances Ann Kilday. Daniel married Margaret Barry at St Edmunds Catholic Church, Collyhurst, Manchester, on 28 May 1904. At the time, he was a caretaker at Stockport Technical School and as a wedding gift, the pair were given a magnificent wall clock, suitably inscribed, by the rest of the staff.

When he enlisted, however, Daniel had become a knife grinder, and Margaret was a box maker at English Sewing Cotton on London Road, where Lithopak now is. The couple had one son, Herbert, who was born in 1906.

As a result of the massive German attack on 21st March 1918, Daniel's battalion was, with many others, involved in a withdrawal over the old Somme battlefields. All the gains that had been made two years earlier at a cost of nearly 420,000 British and Colonial casualties, were lost in a matter of days.

By the 23rd March, the battalion was defending the town of Ham in France, and had been decimated. It was pushed back further and when the town fell, the remnants retired to a position near Eppeville on the southern bank of a canal.

On the morning of the 24th, they were heavily shelled and gradually fell back four miles to another canal - the Canal du Nord. By now they were totally exhausted as they had been fighting continuously for three days and nights, but they continued to be shelled and further withdrawals had to be carried out.

Daniel Kilday died of wounds on the 28th March 1918 at 55 Casualty Clearing Station, Amiens, France, and it is likely that he received these during this period. He is buried at Namps-au-Val Cemetery, approximately 16 kilometres south west of Amiens, in Plot I, Row E, Grave 27. Daniel is remembered in the family as being a very quiet and gentle man. He was 35 years old.

~~~~~~

# 32818 Private Harold Percy **King**
## 1st Bn Kings Royal Lancaster Regiment
## 13 February 1917

When the Battle of the Somme ended, it was not an end to the privations and casualties for the British soldiers. The trenches still had to be manned and shelling and sniping continued. Harold King appears to have been just such a casualty.

Born in Manchester on the 13th February 1893, the son of Mr and Mrs Alfred Percy King, he enlisted into the Kings Royal Lancaster Regiment whilst living with his parents at 'Rostrevor', Queens Road, Hazel Grove. There are no details of his occupation before he joined up.

Over Christmas 1916, the battalion spent the whole of the time in the front line, but from the 1st to the 31st January they were behind the lines either training or providing working parties. On the 1st February, the battalion went back into the front line trenches at Bouchavesnes where, at 5am on the 3rd they were raided by a party of Germans. Although this raid was beaten off, eight men were killed and several were wounded.

From the 5th to the 8th they were relieved by 2nd Bn Lancashire Fusiliers and acted as Brigade Support and then, on the morning of 9th February, they re-entered the same trenches. During the next few days, the battalion received further casualties from both shell and sniper fire.

There are no details of exactly when Harold received his wounds, but it is quite likely that it was during this period. He was then taken to a Military Hospital where, on the 13th February 1917, his 24th birthday, he died.

Harold King was buried at Bray Military Cemetery, very close to the River Somme itself, in Plot II, Row A, Grave 32. his name is also on the Memorial at Norbury Church. After the war, his mother, who was by then a widow, moved to Moss Side, Manchester, which was at that time regarded as one of the better suburbs of Manchester.

~~~~

# 63070 Private Frederick **Leah**
## 9th Bn Welch Regiment
## 15 January 1918

Frederick Leah was born on the 13th July 1898 at 21 Nelson Street, the son of Joseph and Eleanor Leah. Joseph was a spinner and, in view of where he lived, almost certainly worked at the Hollins Mill Co whose mill was only yards from his home. This Company was owned by Ernest Carver who later changed his own and his family's name to Bagshawe. Ernest's son Geoffrey's name is also on the Memorial. Frederick had at least one sibling, a brother named Frank who was born on 14 July 1903.

Frederick was baptised at Norbury Church on 11th August 1898 and in early 1916 he enlisted into the 2/1st Battalion, Pembrokeshire Yeomanry. His stay there did not last for long and he was transferred into the 9th Battalion, Welch Regiment, who were known as The Glamorgan Pioneers. This battalion was the pioneer battalion of the 19th Division and at the time of Frederick's death, it was in the line near Ribencourt, France.

Official records state that Frederick 'died' as opposed to the normal 'killed in action' or 'died of wounds' and this would indicate that he did not die as a result of enemy action. This terminology was used when someone died as a result of an accident (of which there were many) or of illness such as pneumonia, exposure, dysentery etc. There is no indication of the cause of his death and it was not reported in the local paper.

Frederick is buried at Fifteen Ravine British Cemetery, near Villers-Plouich, France, in Plot VII, Row E, Grave 17 and his name is on the Memorial at Norbury Church. He was 19 years old. By 1921 his parents had moved to 29, Nelson Street.

~~~~~

95

# 51556 Private Percy **Le Vesconte**
## 1st Bn Cheshire Regiment
## 25 October 1917

In the 1910 Hazel Grove Directory, Philip J. Le Vesconte was shown as operating a hairdresser's shop at 205, London Road, the site of which is now occupied by the Royal Bank of Scotland.

Percy, his son, was born in Weaste, Salford, about 1894 and joined the Cheshire Regiment in Stockport. The family came to live in Hazel Grove between 1907 and 1910, and by 1921, Philip had died and Percy's mother Florence Jane had gone to live at 16, Sewerby Street, Moss Side, a much more pleasant suburb than it is now.

The 1st Battalion Cheshire Regiment was a regular battalion, but whether Percy was also a regular or had, like many others, been drafted in to replace casualties, is not known. Being a regular battalion it took more than its share of the fighting and for the whole of the war was never out of the front line for more than a month.

On the 26th October 1917, the battalion took part in an attack on Polderhoek as part of the ultimate aim of capturing the village of Passchendaele during the Third Battle of Ypres. Percy was killed the day before and was therefore probably killed on his way up to the front line. On the same day, Allan Holebrook from the same regiment and also from Hazel Grove was also killed. Whether Percy was part of the same Lewis Gun team as Allan and was killed by the same shell which killed Allan is not known. Although Allan Holebrook's death was reported in the local paper, Percy's was not.

Like Allan Holebrook, Percy Le Vesconte has no known grave and his name is on the Memorial Wall at Tyne Cot Cemetery near Ypres, within sight of the village of Passchendaele itself. His name is also on the Memorial at the Methodist Church. He was 23 years old.

Shortly afterwards, the 1st Battalion was sent to Italy.

~~~~~~

# 50956 Private John **Malpass**
## 2nd Bn North Staffordshire Regiment
## 22 June 1919

The 2nd Battalion, North Staffordshire Regiment spent the whole of the War stationed in India but regularly sent drafts to other battalions of the Regiment and received wounded men in return. One of these men was John Malpass. He had originally enlisted in the Transport Section of the R.A.S.C., and was later transferred into the North Staffordshire Regiment.

John had been born on the 24th November 1889, the son of William and Betsy Malpass, who lived at 2, Catherine Street. William was a silk weaver, but by 1910 the family had moved to 42, Mount Pleasant, and he was then a joiner. John and his wife Mary lived at 51, School Street, Cheadle Heath.

In 1919, the battalion was guarding the North West Frontier of India and was stationed near the Khyber Pass. On the 5th May, the Afghan Army invaded India through the Pass and the battalion, along with others, including three battalions of Gurkha Rifles, were sent to Peshawar to help with its defence.

An attack was made on the Afghan forces on May 11th during which the battalion was subjected to heavy machine gun and artillery fire causing the death of five men and wounding 17 others. The Afghans lost over 200 men. On the 22nd June, a picket of 'A' Platoon were suddenly attacked by close range fire, killing two men instantly and two more died of wounds. John was one of the four.

This action was not a part of the Great War, but the people of Hazel Grove decided that despite this, John Malpass should be commemorated on the War Memorial, although his name is slightly misspelt on it. He is also commemorated on the Delhi Memorial, India, the Congregational Church Memorial in the United Reformed Church and the Memorial at Stockport Art Gallery. He was 29 years old.

~~~~~

# 31904 Private Ernest **Marriott**
## 2nd Bn South Lancashire Regiment
## 7 June 1918

Ernest Marriott was born in Windley, near Belper in Derbyshire, but moved to Hazel Grove as a young boy. The 1891 Census shows him to be 11 years old, living at 375, London Road (now part of the Veterinary Surgery), and to be the adopted son of Joseph Marsland, a coal miner and his wife Ann. He attended Norbury School where the Log Book for the Upper School notes that on the 22nd February 1892 he, together with Charles Holebrook took and passed their Labour Certificate Examination in Stockport. Both of them were killed in the war. The 1918 Electoral Roll shows Ernest as an absent voter (he was in the Army) and living on Bramhall Moor Lane (no number given) with his brother Wilfred Marriott, also an absent voter.

In March 1918 the 2nd Battalion, South Lancashire Regiment was, along with many other units, involved in the desperate attempts to stem the German Spring Offensive. This offensive was not totally stopped until August, when the British were able to counter attack leading eventually to the German surrender. In May and June of 1918 however, the end of the war seemed a long way away and the British were still fighting for their lives.

At 1 am on 27 May, the Germans commenced a hurricane bombardment, deluging the British front line and reserve areas. At 4 am German infantry attacked and rapidly overran the forward defences. The 2nd South Lancs were in reserve at Romain, south of St Quentin, France, but at 6.45am were ordered forward to occupy a position at Roucy. The situation was however critical, the Germans having breached the line in several places, though at great loss as the 2nd battalion machine guns cut great swathes through their attackers.

The attacks continued over the next few days and the heavy casualties together with the need for withdrawal reduced the battalion to a handful so that it virtually ceased to exist. Survivors did however fight on with other scattered battalions and it was probably during this desperate and chaotic period that Ernest Marriott received the severe wounds which led to his death on 7 June 1918.

It was possible to evacuate Ernest to a Field Hospital, but his wounds were too severe and he is buried in Epernay French National Cemetery, France, in Grave F15. In addition, his name is on the Memorial at Norbury Church. He was 38 years old.

~~~~

# L/183 Bombardier John William **Marsland**
## 'B' Battery, 150 Brigade, Royal Field Artillery
## 14 July 1916
### (Picture)

The Battle of the Somme claimed the life of another Hazel Grove resident when John Marsland was killed in action on the 14th July 1916.

Before the war, he lived with his parents Charles and Rachel at 313, London Road (now Harries Opticians) and worked for Swain and Co, the owners of the Stockport Advertiser. He was a letterpress printer at their general printing works at King Street East in Stockport where he had also served his apprenticeship, and had worked for the company for 13 years before he volunteered in May 1915. In an obituary for him, the newspaper described him as having 'a quiet but happy disposition and highly esteemed by his employers and those with whom he worked'. He was one of 20 employees of the company who had joined the forces and the second one to have been killed.

As a boy he had attended Norbury School but appears to have not been the best of pupils, the Log Book recording on the 20th June 1894 that he was 'punished for truanting and untruthfulness'. He was however a regular attender at the Methodist Church and on being notified of his death, the Church held a memorial service for him, during which, the newspaper reported, the Dead March from Saul was played.

Shortly after the official notification had been received, John's parents received a letter from his officer in which he stated " He was sent forward to dig a new gun emplacement in a forward position to which the battery was moving. A party of 15 in all were there and everything was very quiet in the evening when suddenly, without warning, a single shell burst on the road amongst them. Only three escaped. Your son was killed instantly. He was buried the same evening close to where he died. Your son only joined the battery recently. He had much hard work to do, digging and building, but he always did his duty conscientiously and cheerfully."

John Marsland is buried at Peronne Road Cemetery, Maricourt, France, in Plot I, Row F, Grave 2. He was 27 years old. Alongside him are the colleagues who were killed by that same shell. Unusually, John shares a grave with another man - Gunner W. Dawson of the same Battery. It would appear likely that the two of them took the full impact of the shell and that it was not possible to tell who was who. John's name is also on the Memorial at the Methodist Church.

~~~~

# 26615 Private John **Martin**
## 1st Bn Cheshire Regiment
## 9 October 1917
(Picture)

Polygon Wood and Sanctuary Wood were two areas outside Ypres which have gone down in history for the ferocity of fighting which went on there during World War 1 and particularly during the Third Battle of Ypres. It was in this area that John Martin lost his life.

Described as "....a good lad at home and well liked by all who knew him", he lived with his parents at 9, Hampson Street. This street no longer exists, but was between the Royal Oak Hotel and Bosden Fold Road, off Commercial Road. John had been born in the locality and before joining up he had worked at Mellors Mill.

On the 3rd October 1917, the battalion went into the area of Poygon Wood and Sanctuary Wood in Divisional Support. The battalion was in reserve during the attack on Broodseinde, but as the attack was a failure it endured considerable shelling whilst in reserve. Only one man in the Battalion was killed on 9 October 1917 - John Martin, by shellfire. Casualties were very high every other day.

His parents received the following letter from an officer in his battalion -
"Dear Mrs. Martin, - It is with great regret that I am only able to inform you of your son's death. We came out of the trenches yesterday and I may mention my first point. It appears that your son was doing signalling duty with his company and was killed instantly on the 8th October (sic). We were able to bury him before coming away. It was with deep sorrow that we laid him at rest. I can assure you my dear Mrs. Martin, by losing your son was one of the greatest blows I have had. He was a fine lad and a good soldier. I liked him; and my signallers and myself especially, wish to extend to you our deepest sympathy in your greatest bereavement. Hoping sincerely that you will soon recover from this terrible blow." The phraseology may seem odd, but no doubt the sentiments were sincere. Although the date of death is given as the 8th in the letter, official Records give it as the 9th.

At the Primitive Methodist Church on London Road on the evening of Sunday 4th November 1917, a memorial service was held for John together with Harry Bowers who had been killed on the same day, but on a different part of the front. Both of them had been regular attenders at the Church and Sunday School.

Although he had been buried at the time, after the war John Martin's grave could not be found and his name is therefore on the Memorial Wall at Tyne Cot Cemetery just outside Ypres. He is also commemorated in the Primitive Methodist Section of the Memorial at the Methodist Church and on the Memorial at Stockport Art Gallery. He was 20 years old.

~~~~~

# 77216 Bombardier Abraham **Mellor**
## 133 Siege Battery, Royal Garrison Artillery
## 9 August 1917

At Christmas 1914, despite the recent start of the war, there was considerable rejoicing at the Primitive Methodist Church on London Road, Hazel Grove. The reason was the marriage of two of its Sunday School teachers, Abraham Mellor and Mary Bennett.

Abraham had been born in Chinley, but for quite some time had lived in Hazel Grove, where he had met and courted Mary Bennett. He worked at Preston's Clothing Stores in Chestergate, Stockport, but all too soon Abraham and Mary were parted when Abraham joined the Army in May 1916 and went to serve in the Royal Garrison Artillery.

In the last week of August 1917, Mary received the impersonal brown envelope notifying her of her husband's death. He had died of wounds in Belgium on the 9th August, having been abroad for twelve months. When and where he was wounded is not known, except that it was in the vicinity of Ypres, and probably during the Third Battle of Ypres.

A Memorial Service was held for him at the Primitive Methodist Church on 2nd September. All the high hopes and expectations of Christmas 1914 were shattered. He was a close friend of the Holebrook family who, a couple of days after the service, received notification of the first of their four family deaths.

Abraham Mellor is buried at Coxyde Military Cemetery, Belgium, in Plot II, Row E, Grave 25, and is also commemorated on the Memorial at the Methodist Church, in the Primitive Methodist section.

~~~~~

# 2664 Lance Corporal Frank **Middlebrooke**
## 6th Bn Cheshire Regiment
## 13 November 1916
(Picture)

When the young men of the village flocked to join the Army in August and September 1914, one of the first to do so was Frank Middlebrooke. He was only 17 when, in September 1914, he left his employment as a hatter at Battersby's Hatworks in Offerton to join the Cheshire Regiment. Clearly he lied about his age in order to get involved in the 'big adventure', but what his parents, Walter and Hannah Middlebrooke of 5, Chapel Houses (off Bramhall Moor Lane) felt about this, we do not know.

From the 13th to the 18th November 1916, the 6th Battalion, Cheshire Regiment was involved in the Battle of Ancre, a small part of the Battle of the Somme. The battalion's activities on November 13th are described in the account on Robert Fenna who died on the same day and was in the same battalion. Suffice to say that, as so often when attacks were ordered in the First World War, the conditions were atrocious with deep cloying mud, rain and shell damage making progress well nigh impossible. Men slipped into flooded shell holes never to be seen again, and to be wounded in more than just the slightest way meant that it was impossible to get back to a dressing station for help. Many wounded men crawled into shellholes to shelter but found that as the rain filled them up, they did not have the strength to pull themselves out. They therefore drowned. The battalion had 167 casualties on that day.

Unlike Bob Fenna, Frank Middlebrooke's body was never found and his name is on the Memorial to the Missing at Thiepval in France, and on the Memorials at the Methodist Church in Hazel Grove and the Art Gallery in Stockport. He was 19 years old.

~~~~~

# 55364 Private Charles **Oldham**
## 'B Coy.' 14th Bn Royal Welch Fusiliers
## 26 December 1918

When the Armistice brought about the end of the war on 11 November 1918, Martha Ann Oldham would not have been as happy as the rest of the population of the village. Her husband Charles had been seriously wounded on 18 September 1918. He had been taken to the 3rd Canadian General Hospital at Boulogne but was too ill to be transported to Britain. Often arrangements were made for the next of kin to visit seriously wounded servicemen in France, but whether or not this happened for Martha Ann is not known.

Charles was the son of James and Sarah Ann Oldham and had been born in Hazel Grove. He enlisted in Stockport and lived with his wife at 22 Hazel Street. Eleven days before Charles died, Herbert Williamson, who lived at 20 Hazel Street, committed suicide at his home because of the wounds he had received, and if Martha had not been with her husband, this cannot have helped her to retain any optimism, however small.

The 14th Battalion, Royal Welch Fusiliers were, like most of the British Army at the time, involved in the final advances leading to the German surrender two months later. On the 18 September 1918, the battalion, along with a number of others, took part in the Battle of Eperhy and in the early morning they formed up for the attack in a downpour of rain through which it was impossible to see farther than a few dozen yards.

A,B, and D Companies carried out the attack with C Company in support. A and D reached their second objective, but B Company was held up by a machine gun. C Company was sent out to support B Company but the battalion had to fall back to its first objective. During the day, Charles Oldham was severely wounded and was taken to a First Aid Post and then on down the line to Hospital.

The wounds proved to be too serious and Charles died on Boxing Day 1918, just over three months after being wounded. He was buried at Turlincthun Cemetery, Boulogne, France in Plot XII, Row E, Grave 4, and was 42 years old. His name is on the Congregational Church Memorial in the United Reformed Church, Short Street.

By 1921 when the War Graves Commission compiled its records, Martha Ann had moved to 30, Gladstone Street, Stockport, but Charles' parents still remained in the village.

~~~~

# 266696 Private Percy **Oldham**
## 9th Bn Cheshire Regiment
## 28 September 1918

By September 1918, the tide had turned for the Allies. The German attempt to break through which started in March 1918 had been halted. The cost in lives was astronomical, but nevertheless, the Germans were now exhausted and had insufficient reserves to make any more progress. The allies counter attacked in August and from then on, the Germans were in retreat until they surrendered in November. They did not give up easily, however, and the Allies incurred very high casualties in the last five months of the war.

Percy Oldham was one of these casualties. The Battalion War Diary gives little information about its activities on the 28th September 1918, stating simply that 11 men were killed from 'D' Coy raiding Neuve Chappelle. Presumably a small party was sent out to raid the German trenches rather than it being a full scale attack, and presumably Percy was a member of that raiding party.

13 years bar one day before he died, on the 29th September 1905, a note in the Log Book of Norbury School remarks that Percy was an 'irregular attender' and that he had only attended on 14 out of 46 possible occasions. Perhaps in 1918 he still had that somewhat cavalier attitude to life and this made him a suitable candidate for a raiding party when he was selected for the one on the 28th September.

His body was never found and his name is therefore on the Memorial to the Missing at Loos, France. He was the son of Mrs. Elizabeth Oldham who, when CWGC records were compiled in 1921, lived at Higher Barn, Macclesfield Road, Poynton, which was a cottage across the road from the junction of Towers Road and Macclesfield Road. In 1918 his address was given as 'Cow Hey Wood'. He was 23 years old and his name is also on the Memorial at the Methodist Church.

~~~~~

# 21038 Private John **Openshaw**
## 6th Bn Queen's Own Cameron Highlanders
## 12 May 1916

When, on the 7th October 1915, Samuel Adshead, John Brown and John Openshaw volunteered into the Cameron Highlanders, they were intent on enjoying an adventure of a lifetime. They enlisted together and travelled to Inverness together. Their service numbers were consecutive. Samuel Adshead and John Openshaw never returned, Samuel being killed after 12 months service and John after only 7 months.

John Openshaw was born in Salford, but had lived in Hazel Grove for some time when he enlisted. He had married Bertha Swindells at Norbury Church on 16 November 1901 when he was 23 and was a 'Finisher', but by the time he joined the Army he was was a butcher and he and his wife lived with his father, also John, a printworker at 7, Smithy Street. His Army record states him to be 36 years 180 days old on enlistment, 5 feet 2 1/2 inches tall and weighing 112 lbs. His service number is consecutive to Samuel Adshead but they were in different battalions. Whether they were split up when they enlisted or at some later date is not known. He was 11 years older than his friend Samuel.

On the 12th May 1916, the 6th Battalion was occupying a former German strongpoint near Loos in Northern France. The 'War History of the 6 Bn Queen's Own Cameron Highlanders' by Norman Mcleod describes the dreadful conditions on the day of John's death as follows:-
"Life in the Hohenzollern Redoubt furnished many ghastly sights and experiences. The line consisted mainly of craters and these were linked up by a system of trenches cut hurriedly from one crater tip to another. Walking through these trenches at night, it was not an unknown experience to be struck on the face by what appeared at first to be the branch of a tree, but on closer scrutiny proved to be a portion of a human arm sticking from the earthen wall and flapping flail-like against every passer by. Such gruesome incident was brought about by the fact that the explosion of a mine frequently buried a whole platoon irretrievably.

In addition to the constant danger of mines, the Hohenzollern Redoubt was the happy hunting ground for snipers, who caused considerable problems and deaths to the Camerons.

At about 4pm on Monday May 11th, the enemy began an intense bombardment of the 13th Royal Scots who were holding the line to the right of the 6th Battalion. This was succeeded by an infantry assault during which the Germans managed to enter the front line over a length of about 500 yards. A platoon of the Camerons immediately set about carrying bombs to the defending troops while two companies were moved up to the reserve trenches. The shelling was heavy and several casualties were suffered at about 1am on the 12th."

John Openshaw's body was never found and he is commemorated on the Memorial at Loos in France as well as the Primitive Methodist section of the Methodist Church Memorial.

~~~~~

# 189588 Driver Edward **Painter**
## 'C' Battery, 245 Brigade, Royal Field Artillery
## 31 July 1920

In addition to the names of men actually killed in the war, the War Memorial contains the names of men who died after it ended, but who in the opinion of the people of Hazel Grove, died as a result of their war service. One such person was Edward Painter.

Born in Manchester, the son of Aaron Weatherall Painter and Annie Painter, Edward, who was known to his friends as 'Teddy', moved to Hazel Grove where, on 23 August 1913, he married Ellen Jackson at Norbury Church. He was 30 years old and a Warehouseman. They had two children - Edna, born on 19 August 1914, who was baptised at Norbury Church on 11 October 1914, despite the fact that Edward and Ellen then lived at 73, Upper Brook Street, Chorlton on Medlock, and Olga, born on 17 October 1916, when the couple lived at 8, Davenport Road, Hazel Grove. In its 1st June 1917 edition, the Stockport Advertiser reported that he was home on leave and 'doing all right' and that he was expecting to go to the front.

The 1919 Voters List shows him to be still in the Army, but when he left the Army he was entitled to a pension, so presumably he suffered some injury or disease during his period of service. He was, however, able to resume work at least for a short period, and was working as a Drapery Warehouseman at the Warehouse of John Rylands & Sons in Manchester up to a short time before his death on 31 July 1920. He was a prominent member of Hazel Grove Conservative Club.

Teddy died of kidney failure. Quite how this is connected with his Army service is not clear, but the people of Hazel Grove were sure that his death was as a direct result of his war service and his name was included on the Memorial and on the Memorial in Norbury Church.

Edward Painter was buried on 3rd August 1920 in Norbury Churchyard, Grave New172 . He was 37 years old.

~~~~~

## 200625 Private Harold Arthur **Percival**  M.M.
## 11th Bn Notts and Derby Regiment (Sherwood Foresters)
## 5 November 1918

Although he was born locally, Harold Percival moved to Belper in Derbyshire in 1906 to work in the English Sewing Cotton Co's works. He lived there with his wife Sarah Jane while his parents, William and Charlotte, continued to live in the village - at 45, Hazel Street. Harold was their youngest son and had attended the Congregational Church and Sunday School as a boy.

Enlisting in his local regiment in 1914, he was based in England for two years and then went to Ireland for a year before going to Italy and then on to France. By early November 1918 everything was going the Allies' way, but German resistance remained. On the morning of the 5th November, the battalion was near Landrecies, to the east of Cambrai in France, and the Battalion War Diary says - "They moved off at 6.15am along with several other units. They fought their way through several villages, encountering heavy machine gun fire. The bridge at Old Mill Des Pres had been blown up and the battalion had to wade through the stream. They pushed on rapidly through Maroilles and prevented the enemy blowing up one of the bridges over the river. Casualties - 1 Officer wounded, 1 O.R. killed, 25 O.R.'s wounded and 1 missing."

The one 'Other Rank' killed was Harold Percival, but the dry comments of the War Diary hide the fact that his bravery that day earned him the Military Medal and cost him his life. His officer wrote to his wife telling her exactly what happened, so we know the precise circumstances under which he died.

" You will have heard of the sad death of your husband, but only I can tell you of the circumstances which led up to it and his great bravery during his last hours on earth. He was my servant, which really means that he was my pal. We ate together, slept together and wherever I went, he went with me. On the morning of 4th November we went into action together - all that day we were fighting and being shelled. On the next day we captured Maroilles and after forcing an entry into the town, found it still occupied by the Huns and at every corner and every house expected them to fire at us. During this very unpleasant fighting your husband was continuously at my side helping me in a hundred different ways. About noon he and I found ourselves alone towards the centre of the town, with six Huns holding a bridge over which we had got to advance. Your husband went back and got two more men and together we rushed forward. The Huns were taken by surprise and, after firing a machine gun at us for a few minutes, cleared off. The bridge was fully mined and but for our rapid advance would have been blown up. I mention this to show that your husband's life was not wasted but that he was wounded whilst nobly doing what it was his duty and mine to do.

When we got to the bridge I ordered two men to cover our advance while your husband and I crossed the bridge. Here your husband shot two Huns and I shot one, reducing their number to three. We went on another 50 yards and then quite suddenly a machine gun fired at us from less than 15 yards. Four bullets struck your husband in the thigh and stomach and he fell. I threw myself down flat and the machine gun continued to fire at us, but by some miracle missed me. About five minutes later the machine gun and Huns cleared off. I then said to your husband - 'I'm going to chance it and have a look at you' but he replied 'Don't be foolish, keep still or they will get you as well.' When I got to him the machine gun started to fire again and again I missed the bullets.

He insisted that we must wait until things quietened down ere he was moved but I was able to get him to a small hollow in the ground where no bullets could get him. I then got hold of some men and advanced again but not before I personally directed the stretcher bearers to your husband.

That was the last I saw of him. On the stretcher he became unconscious and later I found that he died at the Clearing Station the same day. Although I only knew your husband for three days I knew him to be one of the most loyal and brave fellows I ever met. It is but poor consolation to you to receive his MM for by now I suppose you will have received the decoration he so nobly won during his last fight.

I have no ties, no one dependent upon me. Why I should not have been taken and he spared God our Father alone knows."

The writer clearly was not aware of the system. Harold was not formally awarded the Military Medal until the London Gazette announced it on 18th December 1919, one year after he died. There was no formal citation for the award of the MM, but the battalion's records state that it was awarded for his actions on 5th November 1918 when he dashed forward with Pte. Stallebrass to the Maroilles bridge and prevented it from being blown up by the enemy, being severely wounded in the action by machine gun fire.

A memorial service was held at the Congregational Church on Sunday 14th December 1918 and Harold's name was subsequently entered on that Church's Memorial, which is now in the United Reformed Church.

Harold Arthur Percival M.M. is buried at Le Cateau Military Cemetery, France, in Plot V, Row H, Grave 14. He was 36 years old.

~~~~

# Harold **Phillips**

The Commonwealth War Graves Commission has details of 80 men with the initial 'H' or the names Harold or Harry and the surname Phillips. Many have no details other than their regiment and date of death. None has any obvious connection with Hazel Grove. The 1891 Census shows no family of that name living in the village.

During the period 1921 (when the CWGC records were compiled) to the end of 1923 (when the Memorial was built), no person of this name died in England or Wales who can be identified as having any connection with Hazel Grove.

The 1907 and 1910 Hazel Grove Directories both have an entry for Harold Phillips, engineer, at 107, Commercial Road, but whether this is the same man is not known.

The man with the nearest connection is Private Harold Phillips 20206 5th Bn Border Regiment who was born in Manchester and enlisted in Manchester. He was killed in action in France on 10th August 1918 and is buried at Rosieres Communal Cemetery Extension in Plot III, Row E, Grave14. No other information is held about him.

~~~~~

# Henry Barton **Pillatt**
## 21 May 1918

Henry Pillatt was a Boy Scout and, when he died at the age of 16 at his home, 19, Queens Road, the Stockport Express stated that he had died "after 2 months illness contracted in the service of his country".

Born in 1902, the son of Henry Dodsley Pillatt, an Engineering Inspector and Elizabeth McWilliam Pillatt, he was a junior draughtsman at Messrs. Arundel's, Sovereign Works, Stockport. Some years before, he had joined the 1st Davenport BP Scouts where he had risen to become a Patrol Leader.

As a Boy Scout, he had carried out numerous duties and obtained a considerable number of badges. He was known for his enthusiasm and dedication to duty, and went to Cornwall, The Lizard and Penzance on Scout duty in August 1917 and was posted there until December 1917. The Express stated that whilst he was there he "endeared himself to all the officers whose regret was general when through the contraction of a severe cold, he had to relinquish his duties."

In about March 1918, Henry became ill and he died at his home on 21 May 1918, of kidney disease and fluid on the lungs. The latter in particular could well be related to the 'severe cold' which forced him to come back from Cornwall.

Henry's employer was said to 'speak very highly of his character and abilities', and the large number of his workmates at his funeral reflected this.

The funeral itself was a grand affair, many of his scouting colleagues returning from their Whit camp to attend it. The Last Post was sounded at the graveside and an open Marlboro car carried his body in a polished oak coffin, which was covered in the Scout's Union Flag. On this rested his Scout cap.

A very large number of mourners attended, including his parents, grandmother and brothers Frank and Andrew. Andrew, who was born on 22 April 1910, became an apprentice at Mirrlees on 28 November 1927, and Frank was killed in 1943 whilst in the Royal Artillery in World War 2. The family were regular attenders at Norbury Church, but are remembered as not socialising a great deal with the other parishioners.

When the Stockport Advertiser published the first list of names to go on the Memorial on 20 July 1923, Henry's name was included and presumably everybody accepted that his inclusion was correct, because it was inscribed on the Memorial when it was unveiled on 11 November 1923. He was buried at Norbury Church, in grave D503, on 25 May 1918.

# 185161 Private James **Pilsbury**
## 15th Bn Cheshire Regiment
## 28 April 1920

The 15th Battalion, Cheshire Regiment was a 'Bantam' regiment. When recruitment started on a large scale at the beginning of the war, it was realised that a large number of otherwise totally suitable recruits were unable to meet the minimum height limit of 5ft. 4ins. and were as a result being lost to the Army. A movement was set up to rectify this and the main force of this movement came from Alfred Bigland, Member of Parliament for Birkenhead.

Almost singlehandedly, he persuaded the bureaucrats that not only did lack of height not affect a person's ability to be a soldier, but in certain circumstances it was a positive benefit - they were less likely to get shot in the trenches, they needed less clothing and food etc. The regulations were amended in November 1914, and provided that the other medical limits could be met (in fact the chest measurements were increased for the 'Bantams') then any man between 5ft. and 5ft. 4ins was able to join these regiments. Many of the recruits came from the tough mining, shipbuilding and textile towns of Scotland, Wales and the North of England. The very first 'Bantam' regiment in the British Army was the 15th Battalion, Cheshire Regiment of which James Pilsbury was a member.

James was born on 18th February 1887, the son of William and Fanny Pilsbury of 12, Marsland Street. William was a miner in one of the local collieries. James was baptised at Norbury Church on 14th June 1891 and when he was old enough he went to Norbury School. The School Log Book notes that on the 8th March 1900 he was given his 'Half Time Certificate' as he was 13 years old and had regularly attended school. This meant that he now went out to work for half a day and went to school for the other half of the day. He went into the hatting industry.

On 22 November 1914, James enlisted in the Cheshire Regiment, and was therefore one of the first to take advantage of the new regulations enabling him to join the 'Bantams'. He was in France for three and a half years, during which time he was wounded by shrapnel, and hospitalised. Eventually, on 2 February 1919, after the war had ended, he returned to England . Unfortunately he was already showing the early signs of tuberculosis and the Army therefore awarded him a pension. For two months he was able to return to Christy's Hatworks but the illness soon forced him to leave, and despite treatment in a sanatorium, after twelve months illness, he died on the morning of Wednesday 28th April 1920 at the home of his parents, where he had been born 33 years before. The local newspaper reported that the illness had been brought on by "Exposure and hardship in the war, in which he did splendid service".

He was buried at Norbury Church on 1st May 1920 in grave 175, and is commemorated on the Memorial at the same church.

# 31420 Private William **Poacher**
## 8th Bn South Lancashire Regiment
## 21 October 1916

William Poacher has the indignity of having his name wrongly spelt as Porcher on both the War Memorial and the Norbury Church Memorial, but his baptismal entry and the official records all spell his name Poacher.

He was born on 19th July 1889, the son of William and Hannah Poacher of London Road, and on 12th January 1890 he was baptised at Norbury Church. William (senior) was a platelayer on the railway. The 1891 Census shows the family living at 102, Commercial Road and the 1910 Directory shows them living at 32, Brook Street. William (junior) attended Norbury School where the Log book shows that on 19th July 1901, his 12th Birthday, he was struck in the face by Frank Spilsbury, thus drawing blood. Frank Spilsbury was duly punished. On 18 October 1913, William, aged 24 and a platelayer like his father, and still living at 32, Brook Street, married Florence Jessie Dale at Norbury Church. His name was spelt incorrectly on the Marriage Certificate as well, although he signed his name as 'Poacher'. A further problem with his name occurred when their daughter, Gertrude Maude (born 26 July 1916) was baptised at Norbury Church on 10 September 1916, again it was written as 'Porcher'. Their address was given as 5, Station Street, and William was described as a Farm Labourer though, in view of the fact that he was killed less than six weeks later, he was clearly in the Army at the time. The 1918 Electoral Roll shows Jessie living at 224, London Road.

He enlisted in the South Lancashire Regiment in Stockport and after training was posted to France where he took part in the Battle of the Somme. This lasted from the beginning of July to the end of November 1916, but Saturday the 21st October was the final day for William. The day was fine but very cold, and the 8th Battalion along with five others ( including the 13th Cheshires, a member of which was Frank Clough from Hazel Grove, who also did not survive the day) attacked Regina Trench at noon. No Man's Land resembled a morass.

The battalion went forward behind a creeping barrage and reached the trench before the Germans could leave their dugouts. Bombers from the battalion cleared these, but even so, fierce hand to hand fighting took place before Regina Trench was finally in British hands. The battalion bombers went on down another trench, named Stump Road, until they caught up with the British Artillery barrage and could go no further, all the while using their bombs and bayonets to kill about 100 Germans. In addition, they captured another 200.

The battalion's casualties on the 21st October were 26 killed, 91 wounded and 43 missing. The Battalion History states that the high number of 'missing' was 'Probably due to the impetuosity of small groups who pressed on into the maze of trenches beyond their objective. Their exact fate has never been disclosed'. William was one of the 43 and, like Frank Clough, his body was never found. He is therefore commemorated on the Memorial at Thiepval. His name is also on the Memorial at Norbury Church.

~~~~~

# 75089 Private Stanley **Powell**
## 12th/13th Bn Northumberland Fusiliers
## 23 August 1918

The 21st August 1918 marked the beginning of the end for the German Army. On that day, Field Marshal Haig launched his offensive on the exhausted and overstretched enemy. Their Spring 1918 offensive against the British had run out of steam and they had insufficient reserves to continue with it.

At 5.45am on that day, the 12th/13th Bn Northumberland Fusiliers attacked through Beaucourt on the old Somme Battlefield, receiving casualties from both rifle and machine gun fire, but they managed to cross the marshes around the River Ancre. 'C' Coy however, were at first forced back to a nearby railway embankment but in the afternoon fought their way back across the marshes and linked up with 'B' Coy who had managed to stay on the other side. There were 18 casualties in the battalion on that day.

On the 22nd, a number of small enemy raiding parties were repulsed and the battalion counter attacked, but failed to drive the Germans out of the trenches in front of them. On the 23rd therefore, they made another attempt when 'C' Coy sent out a fighting patrol to engage the enemy. No mention is made in the War Diaries of 'Other Rank' casualties, only officers are mentioned, but as official records state that Stanley Powell was killed in action on that day, presumably he was in that patrol. During the period 21 - 29 August 1918, the battalion had 220 casualties.

Stanley was born in Marple, the son of Walter George and Elizabeth Ann Powell. His brothers, Walter and Cyril also served in the forces and the family lived at 8, Grundey Street. Stanley originally enlisted into the Border Regiment, but was later transferred into the Northumberland Fusiliers. He is buried in Connaught Cemetery, Thiepval, France, in Plot VIII, Row G, Grave 9 and his name is also on the Memorial of the Congregational Church, now in the United Reformed Church, Short Street. Robert Fenna, who died nearly two years earlier, is buried in the same cemetery.

~~~~~

# S4/242344 Private George **Ridgway**
## R.A.S.C.
## 26 November 1920

Born on 4 July 1884 at 39, Bramhall Moor Lane, George Ridgway was the son of Thomas (a Railway Labourer) and Sarah Ann Ridgway. His mother had been a widow when she married George's father.

When war broke out, George was 30 and was a butcher in business in Hazel Grove. He is not however shown in the 1910 Directory, so presumably set himself up after that date. George eventually joined the Army Service Corps, but it is not now possible to trace where he was posted. He died of Dysentery, so more than likely he served in Salonika or the Middle East, and on his demob he was awarded an Army Pension indicating that he left the Army with an illness or wound (presumably Dysentery).

George's wife Florence was the eldest daughter of Mr. R. Marginson, who was the licensee of the Finger Post Hotel on Hempshaw Lane and probably had some influence in George's decision to apply for the licence of the Navigation Inn, Woodley. The couple's tenure at the pub was not however very long, because after only a short period, the Dysentery caught up with George and he was taken into Stockport Infirmary where, after only a few days, he died.

Strangely, his address is given on his Death Certificate as 'Hempshaw Lane' and the Church Burial Register gives his address as the Finger Post Hotel. The Notice of Death in the paper however, clearly states 'Navigation Inn, Woodley' as does the report of his death in the local news section.

The date of death was 26th November 1920 and George was buried at Norbury Church on 29th November 1920 in grave CS1. The mourners included his father, two sisters and brothers Tom and Jack. He was 36 years old and had a young child.

The grave no longer exists, but a commemorative stone giving his name and that of three others whose World War 1 graves in the graveyard have been lost, has been erected.

~~~~

# 745040 Driver John William **Ridgway**
## 29 Div. Royal Field Artillery
## 29 September 1918
(Picture)

When Jack Ridgway was born on 11th March 1898, his parents George Herbert Ridgway and Annie Ridgway, were living in a cottage in Cow Hey Wood just inside the Poynton border. George was an engineer, and worked the engine which lowered the cage down into the nearby colliery, which was only a couple of fields away. The family must have had a Hazel Grove connection, however, because Jack was baptised at Norbury Church on 10th April that year and later the family moved to Mill Cottage, Old Mill Lane, Norbury, just across the stream from their old home. Altogether there were six children.

Jack was a particularly adventurous youth and at the age of 16, he joined the RFA. The minimum age for enlisting was 18, and his sister Annie remembers that he was unemployed at the time and somewhat 'at a loose end'. On the morning of 24th January 1915, without telling anyone of his intentions, he went to Stockport and joined the Artillery. His mother and father were naturally very upset at his actions, but accepted his decision. He told Annie that when he arrived to enlist and gave his correct age, the Recruiting Sergeant told him to go outside and come back aged 18. He went out, and returned a few minutes later, telling the same sergeant that he was 18, and was accepted. He didn't have long to wait for his adventures to begin, because in September of that year he was posted to France. He would then have been 17 years old. He was made a driver in an Ammunition Column.

For the next three years he was on active service, at various places in France and Belgium, without getting the slightest injury and was home on leave for 14 days in August 1918. During this leave he was said to be ' bright and enjoying vigorous health'. One month after he returned to the front, he was dead. Whilst returning from transporting ammunition to the front just outside Ypres, he was killed by a German shell.

When the fateful telegram came, Annie remembers that she was working in Argyle Street, but a message was sent for her to return home. She was allowed to have the following day off work. The family later heard that when Jack was buried, he had no personal belongings on him. Whilst lying dead, his body had been looted.

Jack Ridgway was buried in the Menin Road South Military Cemetery, Ypres, Belgium, in Plot II, Row O, Grave 4 and is commemorated on both the Memorials at Norbury Church and at the Methodist Church. He was 20 years old.

# 266505 Private Walter **Ridgway**
## 2nd Bn Cheshire Regiment
## 8 September 1918

Like many other men who lived in Hazel Grove, Walter Ridgway worked in the hatting industry before the war, and also like many others, he worked at Christy's Hatworks in Stockport. He was born in the village, worshipped at the Methodist Church and as a young man had attended their Sunday School. The 1891 Census shows a Walter Ridgway living at 3, Charles Street, the 5 year old son of James (a general labourer) and Sarah A. Ridgway.

Although he was married and had a young daughter he volunteered in early 1915 but stayed in the U.K. until 1st March 1918 when he was posted to the 2nd Battalion, Cheshire Regiment in northern Greece. Regrettably his period of service there was all too short, for within six months he had contracted 'fever' and died of it on 8th September 1918.

His wife Catherine and daughter Mary lived at 215, London Road (now Eurowise Retailers Newsagents) and he was 32 years old. Walter Ridgway is buried at Kirechkoi-Hortakoi Military Cemetery, Thessalonica, Greece, in Grave 52. His name is also on the Memorials at the Methodist Church and at Christy's Hatworks.

~~~~~

# 250869 Private Walter Raymond **Robinson**
## 6th Bn Manchester Regiment
## 14 December 1917

Some records give Walter's second name as Raymond and others as Raywood but it is not known which is correct. He was, however, the younger son of Samuel and Jane Elizabeth Robinson of ' Oakleigh ', Offerton Road, Torkington, and had enlisted into the 5th Reserve Battalion, Manchester Regiment in Manchester. Some time later he was transferred into the 6th Battalion.

Nothing else is known about him except that during a 'quiet' spell in the front line near Givenchy, he was killed by an exploding German shell on 14 December 1917 and was buried in the Gorre British and Indian Cemetery, France, in Plot V, Row A, Grave 25. At the time of his death, Walter was 21 years old. Harry Bowers, who died two months earlier, is buried in the same cemetery.

Walter's brother Harold Sawden Robinson also served in the forces, as a Private in the 8th Bn. Cheshire Regiment, but he survived the war.

~~~~~~

# 17368 Rifleman Frederick **Rowbotham**
## 12th Bn Kings Royal Rifle Corps
## 18 August 1916
(Picture)

Born on 22 January 1896 at 62, Commercial Road, Frederick Rowbotham lived there all his short life until he enlisted in the Kings Royal Rifle Corps. He was the son of Joseph and Elizabeth Rowbotham and Joseph was a hatter. Baptised at Norbury Church on 10 May 1896, Frederick had attended Norbury School where on 13 January 1903 the Log Book records him as off sick, suffering from 'Brain Fever'. Although he recovered, his sister Catherine was not so lucky and died on 12th February 1903 of pneumonia.

The family were regular attenders at the Primitive Methodist Church where Frederick attended the Sunday School and was a member of the choir. He was such a regular attender that he had been at church with his fiancee Florrie on his last Sunday at home.

Frederick was killed whilst taking part in the Battle of the Somme. On 6th August, his battalion relieved another in the front line trenches to the north of the town of Albert. They remained there until 14th August. All the while the enemy was active with rifle grenades and trench mortars, particularly on the evening of the 10th when they bombarded the British trenches heavily with mortars and shells of every description.

On 14th August, they were relieved and marched to Divisional Reserve at Couin, about nine miles to the east of Doullens, but they were soon ordered to leave there and on the 18th they marched to Candas where they were to entrain to go back into the line at Guillemont. During this march, they were shelled and Frederick Rowbotham was killed.

A memorial service was held for him on Sunday 23rd September 1916 at the Primitive Methodist Church, during which several people, including Samuel Penny, who was a well known character in the village, said a few words and expressed their sympathy to Frederick's parents, brothers, sisters and fiancee. He was a well liked and respected member of the congregation.

Frederick Rowbotham is buried at Caterpillar Valley Cemetery, Longueval, France, in Plot X, Row G, Grave 12 and his name is in the Primitive Methodist section of the Memorial at the Methodist Church. He was 20 years old.

~~~~

# 126076 Private Harold **Skeen**
## 3rd Bn Machine Gun Corps (Infantry Section)
## 15 May 1918
(Picture)

Coal was vital to the war effort. Not only did it 'keep the home fires burning', but at the time of the Great War, electricity was generated by it, gas extracted from it, and the main means of power - steam - was provided by it. The machines which made the armaments were fuelled by steam. Trains and battleships were powered by it, and as petrol engines were still in their infancy, a considerable amount of motorised transport depended on it. In short, the war could not be run without it. It was so vital that when conscription was introduced in February 1916, miners were exempted from being called up. Harold Skeen was a miner.

One of the more unpalatable aspects of the behaviour of civilians during the war was the way that some women pursued any man who was not in uniform and tried to humiliate him into joining up. It got so bad that servicemen who had been discharged wounded, had to be given special badges to stop them being harangued in this way. Even servicemen at home recuperating from wounds had to be given special uniforms.

The family remembers that Harold, a strapping young miner, was constantly the subject of this type of attention, despite the vital nature of his work. He was presented with white feathers (the sign of cowardice), and was regularly the subject of taunts and harrassment. It was too much for a boy of 18 to cope with, and despite the fact that he did not have to, he enlisted in the Kings Shropshire Light Infantry. Later, he transferred into the Machine Gun Corps and was with them near Cambrai when, on the morning of 21 March 1918, the Germans launched their massive Spring Offensive.

On 22 March, Harold received a gunshot wound to his thigh which broke the bone and he was therefore unable to get away from the German advance. As a result he was captured and was transported to a Prisoner of War Camp at Niederzwehren, 10 kms south of Kassel in the middle of Germany. He arrived there on 4 April 1918 but, as these were the days before antibiotics, blood poisoning set in. He was unable to fight it and died in the camp hospital at 5pm on 15 May 1918.

Harold was born on 19th June 1897 at 3, Charles Street, the son of John and Caroline Skeen. John was a labourer. Harold was baptised at Norbury Church on 28th February 1900 and by 1910, the family had moved to 11, Newtown Street. Harold's brother John Thomas Skeen also served in the forces and survived, and in 1920, after John's wife Florence gave birth to a son, they named him Harold after his uncle. The name appears to have been fated, for young Harold was called up during World War 2, and on 21 September 1944 he too died in the service of his country, whilst also a prisoner, this time of the Japanese who, during World War 1 had been allies of the British, but were enemies in World War 2.

Harold (Senior) was buried at Niederzwehren Cemetery, Germany, in Plot X, Row B, Grave 11 and his name is on the Memorial at the Methodist Church. He was 20 years old.

~~~~~

# 5316 Sergeant Walter **Smith**
## 11th Bn Lancashire Fusiliers
## 22 March 1918

The local newspapers carried no report of the death of Walter Smith and with a surname as numerous as his, it has been difficult to ensure that details of the correct person have been obtained.

No trace has been found of anyone of this name with an obvious connection with Hazel Grove, but a distinct possibility is Walter Smith who was born in Disley and who, whilst living in Stockport, enlisted in the Lancashire Fusiliers in Ashton under Lyne. The 1910 Hazel Grove Directory shows a W. Smith, painter, living at 13, Wesley Street and the 1918 Voters List shows a Walter Smith who was serving in the forces at the time, at 13, High Street, Hazel Grove.

Walter was killed in action on the second day of the German Spring Offensive of 1918. This massive assault on the British lines, just where they were at their weakest, drove a large hole in the British front, causing enormous casualties and the loss of virtually all of the gains won in such a costly manner during the previous two years. The 11th Battalion was in the line at Fremicourt and at 5am on the 21st March, the Germans launched a heavy barrage. This forced the Fusiliers into a defensive position to the south of the Bapaume - Cambrai road, 1000 yards north of Lebucquiere. They were forced to link up shell holes in order to gain shelter.

At 2.15pm on the following day, the 51st Highland Division attempted a counter attack which failed and this resulted in another German attack which again forced the battalion to withdraw, this time under the cover of darkness. In the period 21st - 28th March, the battalion lost 23 men killed and 92 missing.

Walter Smith was one of these and his body was never found. His name is therefore on the Memorial to the Missing at Arras in France and on the Memorial at the Art Gallery in Stockport.. The CWGC have no details of any next of kin.

# 11164 Sergeant Gilbert William **Stanton**
## 1st Bn Royal Welch Fusiliers
## 16 May 1915
### (Picture)

Gilbert Stanton came from a military family. He himself was a regular soldier, having gone to Chester and joined the Cheshire Regiment in 1907. During the war, if not before, his three brothers were also in the Army.

All the boys went to Norbury School, but the family seems to have moved at some time to Stockport, where his parents James and Harriet Alice lived in Higher Hillgate and his sister Florence Mottershead lived at 1, Harrop Street. After joining the Army, Gilbert went out to India for seven years and just before the outbreak of hostilities he was transferred into the Royal Welch Fusiliers. From India he went to France and managed to get a short period of leave around the end of 1914, which he spent in Stockport with his friends and family. He was not married and was 28 years old when he was killed.

Zero hour for the Battle of Festubert was 3.15am on 16 May 1915, and although it was extremely dark the battalion managed to get across No Man's land, despite heavy enemy shelling. They forded a small river but when they reached the German front line, they found that, despite the two day British bombardment, little damage had been done. In fact, many British shells had been duds and the furore about this back home after the battle, together with the fact that there was a great shortage of shells, resulted in Lloyd George becoming Minister of Munitions.

No Man's Land was only 120 yards wide at this point and because of heavy machine gun fire the men thinned out very rapidly, before they jumped into the German trenches and engaged in half an hour's strenuous hand to hand combat in a frightful tangled system of trenches. During this trench fighting, the Company Sergeant Major acted in such a way that he was later awarded the Victoria Cross. Gilbert Stanton, however, did not survive it.

Shortly after receiving notification of his death, Gilbert's parents received a letter from one of his friends, Lance Corporal Cabman, in which he said -
"Just a few lines to let you know that Sergeant Stanton got killed while in action. We were making a charge upon the German trenches and he was shot through the head. He was our leader. We miss him very much, as he was so well liked among our company. You will have read in the papers about the work we are doing; advancing under great difficulties for about three miles and making the Germans run. We don't give them much mercy for we remember what we have suffered at their hands. I hope you will let his friends know, as he wanted this to be done if anything happened while he made the advance."

After the war, Gilbert Stanton's body could not be found and his name is therefore on the Memorial at Le Touret, Pas de Calais, France, as well as being on the Memorial at Norbury Church.  Of 25 officers and 806 other ranks who started  the battle that day, only 6 officers and 247 other ranks came out of it.

~~~~~

# 5469 Private Bertram Clarke **Stead**
## 18th Bn Australian Imperial Force
## 3 May 1917

Bertram Stead was the son of Walter Reynolds Stead, a tram driver, and Mary Louisa Stead. He was born on 10th January 1889 at their home, 10, Bramhall Moor Lane and was baptised at Norbury Church on 27th March 1903, when he was 14 years old. His two brothers, Alfred Alexander, who was born on 4 August 1891, and Walter Barrymore, born on 25 June 1896, were also baptised on that same day.

When he grew up, Bertram became a carpenter and at some time, it is not known when, he emigrated to Australia, settling in Auburn, New South Wales, although his parents remained in Hazel Grove. On 2nd March 1916, at the age of 27, he decided to enlist, giving his address as Princes Road, Auburn, and stating that his wife's name was Alice Jane Stead. Whether they married before leaving England or whether they met in Australia is not known. He authorised the deduction of two fifths of his pay to be paid to his wife and his record sheet shows him to have been 5ft. 7ins. tall, weighing 8st 10lbs, 31ins. chest, light brown hair, grey eyes and a fair complexion. He also had a scar on the back of his left hand. Possibly this came from an accident while carrying on his trade as a carpenter.

Bertram joined 'M' Coy. of the Depot Battalion at Camp in Bathurst on 16th March 1916 to start his training and on 22 August 1916 he left Sydney on the "Wiltshire" to take part in the war. The ship arrived in Plymouth on 13th October 1916 and more training was carried out until, on 13th December 1916, he left Folkestone for France on the "Princess Henrietta". A spell completing his training at the notorious base camp in Etaples followed. This camp was known for the brutality of the instructors and for the needless indignities heaped upon the soldiers sent there. Towards the end of the war, there was in fact a small mutiny there and it was where the activities of the "Monocled Mutineer" of subsequent TV fame took place.

Leaving Etaples on 26th January 1917, Bertram joined the 18th Battalion, Australian Infantry Division, but his time with them was all too short for, on 3rd May 1917, he was posted "Missing". Efforts were always made to try to find out what had happened to missing men and on 27th August 1917, Private C.F.Adams made out the following statement - " I saw Pte Stead B.C. hit in the temple on 3rd May 1917. He fell into a deep shell hole. When walking back myself wounded, I noted he was still there and had bled profusely from the temple. He was undoubtedly dead and had been moved since being hit. He was in the same platoon as I was."

It was not until 5th November 1917 that Alice Stead was informed that her husband had definitely been killed and on 29th August 1918 she wrote to Army HQ asking that 'anything belonging to the late Pte B.C.Stead' be forwarded to her. A pension of £2 per fortnight was granted to her and £1 per fortnight to their daughter Marie Audrey and on 5th October 1922 Alice acknowledged receipt of Bertram's Victory Medal,

British War Medal and Memorial Scroll and King's Message.On 28th December 1922 she acknowledged receipt of his Memorial Plaque. Bertram was 28 years old.

Bertram Stead's body was not recovered and he therefore has no known grave. He is commemorated on the Australian Memorial at Villers Bretonneaux in France. Alice and Marie stayed in Australia, but when a grateful Government offered them a copy of the entry on the Memorial at a cost of 3 shillings (15p) in 1923, they could not afford it. Bertram's name is also on the Memorials at Norbury Church and Stockport Art Gallery.

~~~~~

# 26012 Private George **Stubbs**
## 2nd Bn Duke of Wellington's Regiment
## 15 April 1918
### (Picture)

On volunteering for the Army in Manchester in October 1915, George Stubbs was able to stipulate which unit he wished to go to and, being very interested in motor cars, he went into the Army Service Corps as a motor vehicle driver.

His parents Samuel and Sarah lived at 165, London Road (now Edward Mellor, Estate Agents) from where Samuel ran his business as a coach proprietor, but George worked as a car driver for a Mr. Potts of Marple who, like George's father, ran a coach business. Possibly they were business colleagues and Mr. Potts agreed to employ his friend's son.

George, who was born in Hazel Grove, was a regular attender at the Wesleyan Church and was a member of the Young Men's Class, but his great interest was cricket. He was a prominent playing member of the Wesleyan Cricket Club and regularly took the local children to various cricket matches on the back of his horse and cart.

In early 1916 George was sent to France, but on 14th October 1917 he was transferred into an infantry regiment - The Duke of Wellington's Regiment (West Riding Regiment). By this time, there was a massive shortage of infantrymen - probably due to the high casualty rates. Two weeks later he obtained two weeks leave, from the 2nd to the 16th November, which was spent in the U.K. It was to be his last, for on the 5th December 1917 he was gassed and admitted to 8 Casualty Clearing Station. From there he was moved to 10 Field Hospital on 7th December and to 6 Stationary Hospital on 13th December. Another move came on 4th January 1918 when he was sent to 57 Casualty Clearing Station and then on to F Depot on 12th February. Finally on 19th February he was considered fit enough to return to the front with his unit. On the 15th April 1918 he was killed.

On the 14th April the Battalion relieved another on the bank of the La Bassee canal to the north of Bethune in France and on the following day, together with the 1st Royal Warwicks, crossed the canal to attack Pacout Wood. The operation was not a success. 35 men were killed, 185 wounded and 7 missing.

George was buried at Chocques Military Cemetery, France, in Plot III, Row D, Grave 23 and his name is on the Memorial at the Methodist Church. George was 26 years old and unmarried. Also buried in the same cemetery is George Tallent who died six days earlier.

~~~

# 52950 Private James **Swindells**
## 22nd Bn Manchester Regiment
## 4 October 1917

Although he was born in Hazel Grove, James Swindells lived at 82, Florist Street, Stockport with his parents James and Isabella and also his brother William, when war broke out. The parents were to lose both their sons in the next four years.

The 22nd Battalion, Manchester Regiment was one of the 'Pals' Regiments, recruited from the many men who had either grown up together or had worked together and wished to remain together when they joined the Army. This encouraged recruitment considerably, but was to have devastating consequences when the battalions were involved in a battle and losses were high. Whole neighbourhoods of young men were virtually wiped out.

James was yet another casualty of the Third Battle of Ypres. The battalion had taken heavy casualties during the Battle of the Somme, but it is not known whether James had fought his way through that or was a replacement to fill the enormous gaps left in its ranks.

On 2nd October 1917, the Battalion moved up towards the front near Broodseinde and spent the evening in some filthy dugouts on a railway embankment to the west of Zillebeke Lake. At 9.30pm on the following day, they marched to an assembly point in Polygon Wood ready to make their attack.

At 6am in the early dawn on the 4th, under dreadful weather conditions of torrential rain and atrocious ground conditions, the attack started and they advanced towards their objective. The battalion on their right failed to keep up, with the result that by about 8.10am they were being enfiladed by machine gun fire causing heavy casualties. Fortunately, British Artillery fire prevented a counter attack by the Germans but their position was precarious throughout the day and following night. During that day, the Battalion had a total of 288 casualties. They were not relieved until the 7th October.

James's parents were informed that he was missing and like many thousands in their position they clung to the hope that he might still be alive. In the 3rd January 1918 edition of the Stockport Express, they inserted an advertisement asking that if anyone had any information about him, they should contact his parents at Florist Street.

It was not to be. James's body was never found and his name is on the Memorial Wall at Tyne Cot Cemetery, near Ypres in Belgium. He is also commemorated on the Memorial at the Stockport Art Gallery.

# 59805 Private William **Swindells**
## 10th Bn Northumberland Fusiliers
## 28 October 1918

Twelve months after his brother James was killed, William Swindells died of wounds in Italy. Two weeks later, the war ended.

The son of James and Isabella Swindells, he was born in Hazel Grove but the family was living at 82, Florist Street, Stockport, when the war broke out. The 1891 Census shows the family living at 19, Newtown Street with James being a hatter. William was 5 years old but there was no mention of his brother James. Presumably he was not yet born. The 1907 Hazel Grove Directory shows the family to be living at 45, Bramhall Moor Lane, but they appear to have moved by 1910 as they are not shown in the Directory for that year. The family connection with Hazel Grove remained, however, because by 1921 James and Isabella had returned to the village and on 12th June 1939, Isabella was buried in Norbury Churchyard.

William enlisted in the Northumberland Fusiliers in Manchester and went with them to Italy to shore up the flagging Italians against the Austrians. The Battalion was involved in fighting around the River Piave, about 20 miles north of Venice, desperately trying to halt the collapse of the Italians and the capture of the city.

At about 8pm on the 26th October they took up their position as Brigade Reserve and on the next morning followed the 11th Battalion, Northumberland Fusiliers as they attacked at 6.45am. Despite being the reserve, they took over 50 casualties from machine gun fire enfilading from the left. At 12.30pm on the 28th, they attacked again, capturing numerous enemy machine guns though again taking heavy casualties.

There is no indication of when William was wounded, but it is quite likely that it was during one of these few days. On the day William died, the 28th, Private Wilfred Wood of 52, Chester Road, who was in the same battalion, won the V.C. for single handedly capturing an enemy strongpoint.

William is buried in Giavera Cemetery, Italy, in Plot III, Row E, Grave10. He was 33 years old.

~~~~~

# 202384 Private George **Tallent**
## 4th Bn South Lancashire Regiment
## 9 April 1918
### (Picture)

Winson Houlgate Tallent and his wife Alice of 44, London Road had five sons, all of whom served in the Army during the war. Three of them, John, Godfrey and Frank survived. The couple married on 16 July 1887 at Norbury Church when Winson, a salesman, was 28 and his bride Alice Charlton was 20. In 1894, however, Winson was described as a 'manufacturer'.

The family seem to have moved around, being on various occasions in Clitheroe, Macclesfield and Hazel Grove, but the boys were baptised at Norbury Church so their ties to the village remained strong. George was born in Clitheroe on 15th December 1893, but his parents brought him to Norbury Church on 15th April 1894 to be baptised and he spent his youth in the village, moving to Macclesfield some time before the war started, but the family were back in Hazel Grove by the end of the war. Educated at Macclesfield Grammar School, George had been employed by a firm of Chartered Accountants in King Street, Manchester before enlisting. At the time of his death he was an acting Corporal and had been recommended for a commission.

The 4th Battalion, South Lancs. were involved in the desperate attempts to hold the German Spring 1918 Offensive and on 8 April 1918 they moved to Locon and Essars, suffering 33 casualties from shell fire and gas. The morning of 9th April dawned fine but misty and just after 4am the whole Divisional front was bombarded, but an infantry attack did not develop until 9am when the mist had lifted a little, although visibility was still limited to 20 or 30 yards. Using this as cover, the enemy crept close to the Battalion's positions before they were discovered. It was then found that the Portuguese on the Battalion's left had been virtually destroyed by the enemy barrage, with the result that the South Lancs. had no protection on their left.

Together with other units they tried to plug the hole in the defences, but the Germans were pouring through it and it was with great difficulty that the line was restored. During the day, the Battalion lost 16 killed and 65 wounded. George Tallent, who was 24 years old, was killed in action that day and is buried at Chocques Military Cemetery, near Bethune, France, in Plot IV, Row C, Grave 29. His name is also on the Memorials at Norbury Church and at Macclesfield Grammar School. Also buried in the same cemetery is George Stubbs who died six days later.

# 705622 Gunner Winson **Tallent**
## 'C' Battery 275 Brigade Royal Field Artillery
## 10 May 1918
### (Picture)

Four weeks after notification of George's death, Alice Tallent was notified of the death of her son Winson. He had been one of the very first to join up, having enlisted in Manchester on 2 September 1914.

Named after his father, he was baptised at Norbury Church on 19 May 1889, when family was living in Station Street, Hazel Grove. He was brought up mainly in Hazel Grove but was living in Macclesfield when the war started. In the report of his death in its 31st May 1918 edition, the Stockport Advertiser described him as having 'a pleasant countenance and engaging manner which endeared him to everyone he came into contact with.'

After he enlisted, his first foreign posting was to Egypt but he was later transferred to France where he was gassed during the Third Battle of Ypres in Autumn 1917 and invalided back to England. On recovery he went back to France on 27 March 1918 and beyond a note written the next day announcing his arrival, nothing further was heard of him until his mother received a letter from his battery commander informing her of Winson's death from wounds. Apart from the fact that his battery was attached to the 55th Division there is no indication of where it actually was when he was wounded. Like his brother George however, he would have been involved in the retreat from the German Spring Offensive of 1918.

Winson Tallent has no known grave and is commemorated on the Memorial at Loos in northern France as well as the Memorial at Norbury Church. He was 29 years old.

Three brothers survived the war. Sergeant John Tallent had been in the Anti-Aircraft Forces in France, Second Lieutenant Frank Tallent was also in the RFA but was invalided out at Christmas 1915 and the youngest brother Godfrey, who emigrated to Australia in 1913, joined the Australian Forces and served with them in Gallipoli but was discharged wounded. He recovered and rejoined the Anzac Motor Transport Section in France.

# 419637 Sergeant Edward Hammond **Taylor**
## Cameronians (Scottish Rifles)
## 20 July 1919

Born on 1st September 1892 at 21, Chester Road, Edward Taylor was the son of Edward Hammond Taylor and Lucy Florence Taylor. Edward (Senior) was a butcher. In the 1910 Directory of Hazel Grove, Edward (Senior) is shown as being at 7, John Street, but this is most probably the family home rather than his shop. The family also lived in Hatherlow Lane at one time, but by the end of the war they had moved to 15, Oxford Street, Heaton Norris. Edward (Junior) was baptised at Norbury Church on 2nd October 1892.

Edward was severely wounded during the war, but no information can be traced as to where or when. He was, however, invalided home and sent to Wharncliffe Hospital, Sheffield, where after a long period he eventually succumbed to his injuries on 20th July 1919. During his spell in the hospital he was, presumably for administrative reasons, transferred into the Labour Corps.

The body of Edward Hammond Taylor (Junior) was brought to Hazel Grove where, on Saturday 25th July 1919 he was buried in Norbury Churchyard in grave DC188. He is commemorated on the Memorial at Norbury Church, and together with three other World War 1 casualties, his name is on a special commemorative stone in the front of the Churchyard as the original graves are no longer marked. He was 26 years old and his brother John Taylor was also killed in the war.

~~~~~

# 2760 Private Frederick **Taylor**
## 6th Bn Cheshire Regiment
## 29 August 1916
### (Picture)

Another man who enlisted very early in the war was Frederick Taylor of 95, Chapel Street. He was also one of the many from the village to be killed on the Somme.

As a child, Frederick had attended Norbury School and Sunday School and before the war he was employed by Hollins Mill Co. but on the 3rd October 1914 he went to Stockport and enlisted in the Cheshire Regiment.

Between the 23 July and 3 September 1916, the Battalion was taking part in the Battle of The Somme, and was in the trenches at Hamel in front of Thiepval. On the morning of 29th August, a day when the temperature eventually reached 82F and there was heavy rain, the trenches were shelled by the Germans. Frederick was a stretcher bearer and while he was moving through the trenches to assist some of the wounded men, a shell landed near him and killed him outright. He was 24 years old.

The Battalion's War Diary for the day simply says, " In the line at Le Hamel, north of Thiepval. Enemy shelling demolished the trenches, killing 1 O.R." That 'Other Rank' was Frederick Taylor.

Frederick was buried at Hamel Military Cemetery, near the town of Albert in France in Plot I, Row A, Grave 40 and his name is also on the Memorial at Norbury Church. By 1921, Frederick's mother Annie, who was a widow, had moved to 2, Commercial Road.

~~~~

# 20975 Private Harold **Taylor**
# 3rd Bn Coldstream Guards
# 11 October 1917

Harry Taylor enlisted in the Coldstream Guards on 8 December 1915 in Stockport. He was a brickmaker aged 34 and was 5ft. 10ins. tall. Unfortunately, his total length of service was only 1 year 308 days. His total length of married life was only 1 year 305 days and few of them were actually spent with his wife Annie Mabel (May) Oldham, aged 28, whom he married at Norbury Church on 11 December 1915, three days after he enlisted.

Harry was the son of Mrs. S. Taylor of 264, Buxton Road, Great Moor, but after their marriage he and his wife lived at 24, Neville Street. May had lived at 53, Hazel Street, before their marriage. Originally he was posted to the 5th Battalion which was a training battalion but was posted to the 2nd Battalion on 14th December 1916 and then on 12th September 1917 he was transferred to the 3rd Battalion.

Both the 2nd and 3rd Battalions were part of the 1st Guards Brigade and were fighting together outside Ypres during the Third Battle of Ypres. The Stockport Express, when announcing his death, says that 'He had only been out one month' which ties in with the period he had been in the 3rd Battalion but does not fit in with the fact that the 2nd Battalion was also in Belgium and had been for some time. Possibly there was a small section still in the UK.

All the official records and the newspapers state that Harry was 'accidentally killed whilst on active duty' but there is no record of what actually happened to him. Thursday 11 December was a cloudy day, with the temperature reaching a maximum of 50F and about 1/4 inch rainfall. The 1st Guards Brigade were to the south of Houthulst Forest, north east of Ypres. Two days before, they had been involved in an attempt to get into the forest and had encountered fierce rifle fire from the Germans in the forest but managed to reach their objective. No activity of any significant kind is recorded for the Battalion on the 11th so it is not possible to deduce what actually happened to him.

No body was found after the war. If he had been buried at the time, the grave was subsequently lost and Harry's name is therefore on the Memorial Wall at Tyne Cot Cemetery outside Ypres. He was 37 years old. His wife, May, collected his Victory Medal in 1921.

~~~~~~

# 160873 Gunner John **Taylor**
## 299 Siege Battery, Royal Garrison Artillery
## 21 March 1918

On the day the Germans launched 'Operation Michael', the code name for their Spring 1918 Offensive, they managed to force the British Army into full retreat, scattering units, destroying artillery, killing many hundreds and capturing many others. The British Army was in total chaos for that and many subsequent days.

Twenty men from Hazel Grove were killed before the tide was turned, even more than died during the Battle of the Somme. John Taylor was killed on the very first day of the retreat. Being part of the RGA he would probably have been in the crew of a large gun and therefore some distance behind the lines, but it has not been possible to find out where he was, or precisely what happened to him. Being well behind the lines it is very likely that his position was hit by a German shell. Things would have been very hectic indeed on that day, so even if it had been possible to bury him, it would have been a hasty affair. After the war it was not possible to trace any grave for him.

John was the eldest son of Edward Hammond Taylor, a butcher, and Lucy Florence Taylor and was the older brother of Edward Hammond Taylor (Junior) who died as a result of his wounds in July 1919. He was baptised at Norbury Church on 11 June 1882 and attended Norbury School. In the School Log Book there is an entry dated 10 May 1895 to say that John left that day to take up full time work - he was 13. The family lived at 21, Chester Road.

On 17 December 1906, when he was 24, he married Jessie Elizabeth Little at Norbury Church and gave his address as 2, Vine Street. On the Marriage Certificate, his occupation was given as 'Butcher', so clearly he followed in his father's footsteps. The couple produced four children and in 1921 Jessie and the children lived at 16, Greg Street, Reddish.

As no grave was ever found, John Taylor's name is on the Memorial at Arras in France. He was 36 years old. His name is also on the Memorial at the Stockport Art Gallery.

~~~~

# 2375 Private Emrys **Thomas**
# 7th Bn Manchester Regiment
# 20 July 1915

Although his name is not on the Memorial and he was not a native of Hazel Grove, Emrys Thomas was living in the village when he enlisted in the Manchester Regiment shortly after the outbreak of the war.

Emrys was born on 30 June 1895 in Caernarvonshire, the son of William Griffiths Thomas, a Corn Merchant, and Margaret Elizabeth Thomas of 'The Moorings', Llanbedlig, Caernarvon. They remained there when he moved to Hazel Grove, to start work on 28 March 1912 as an apprentice at Mirrlees. He was 16 years old and lodged at 88, Bramhall Moor Lane. Once in the village, he joined the Congregational Church and became a member of their 'Young Men's Class' so, when the information came through that he had been killed, the church held a special and well attended Memorial Service for him on Sunday 1 August 1915, during which the Rev. G.M.Jenkins gave an 'impressive and sympathetic address' and special hymns were sung.

The 7th Battalion, Manchester Regiment was a Territorial Battalion, which was embodied in the first few days of the war. Emrys joined the battalion on 1 September 1914, which would indicate that he was in the Territorial Army before the war. On 10 September 1914 the battalion sailed for Egypt where it remained until 2 May 1915 when it moved to Gallipoli, landing on the 7th. It was involved in the disastrous campaign there, taking many casualties. On 11 May it entered the trenches and on the following day received its baptism of fire. On 5 July 1915 it helped to repulse a fierce attack on the Division on its left, killing about 150 Turks. There were further small actions resulting in many casualties, though on which day Emrys Thomas was severely wounded is not known. He was evacuated to Alexandria Hospital, Alexandria, Egypt, where he died on 20 July 1915.

Emrys was buried in the Alexandria (Chatby) Military Cemetery, Egypt, in Grave K133 and although his name was not included amongst those inscribed on the War Memorial, it is on the Congregational Church Memorial, situated in the United Reformed Church, Short Street. He was 20 years old.

~~~~~

## 49873 Private William **Tierney**
## 9th Bn Cheshire Regiment
## 21 November 1916

Although the Battle of the Somme is generally regarded as having petered out in the mud, rain and morass by 19th November 1916, the killing did not stop. The trenches still had to be manned, raids carried out and the enemy harrassed. Unfortunately, the Germans felt the same way and casualties therefore continued on both sides. It is calculated that in total, more men were killed during these so called 'quiet' periods than in actual set piece battles.

William Tierney seems to have been one such casualty. By 21st November the succession of British attacks had ceased and winter had set in to add to the miseries of the troops. The 9th Battalion was in the vicinity of Ancre Heights in the area of the Somme, manning trenches near the former German strong point called 'Stuff Redoubt'. The mud was thigh deep, making life virtually impossible. It took all a man's strength simply to stay alive. Sleep was nearly impossible, for to lie down and sleep meant the distinct risk of sinking into the mud and drowning. The trenches themselves regularly collapsed because the walls turned into mud and they had to be constantly repaired. Men slept wherever they could find a ledge out of the rain and mud.

18 year old William Tierney just disappeared. The War Diary entry for 21st November 1916 simply says 'In dug out, not in action. No casualties.' The official records however, all clearly say that he was killed in action on 21st November. There is a discrepancy here which cannot now be cleared up, but whatever happened to him, his body was never found.

William was the son of James and Eliza Tierney of 6, Buxton Road. James was the village Optician. William is commemorated on the Memorial to the Missing at Thiepval, France and on the Memorial at Norbury Church, where the family were regular attenders.

~~~~~

# 242740 Private George Arthur **Vernon**
## 5th Bn Royal Welch Fusiliers
## 15 April 1917

The liner 'Arcadian' was built for The Royal Mail Steam Packet Company in 1899 by Vickers & Sons. She was 500 feet long, weighed 8939 tons and was capable of a maximum speed of 15 knots. She saw service in the company's trade until she was requisitioned by the War Office at the beginning of the First World War and converted into a troopship.

On Sunday 15 April 1917, the ship, with a complement of 1335 crew and troops, under the command of Captain C.L. Willats was sailing from Salonika to Alexandria. She had come out from England bringing reinforcements to the Eastern theatres of the war, and having dropped off those destined for Salonika, was continuing onwards to take the remaining men to Palestine when, without warning at 5.45pm she was torpedoed in the southern Aegean, 26 miles NE of Milos. Several lifeboats were destroyed in the explosion. Fortunately, the troops on board had just completed a boat drill and this was a major factor in the saving of 1058 of its passengers and crew.

It is very likely that even more could have been saved were it not for the fact that the ship suddenly capsized and in addition, a considerable amount of wreckage was sucked down with the ship and then came to the surface with great force, killing many who were swimming in the sea. It took only six minutes for the ship to sink and as a result, the high number saved is quite exceptional.

Of the 277 men lost, 19 were army officers, 214 were other ranks, 10 were naval ratings and 34 were crew. One of the 'other ranks' was Arthur Vernon who lived with his parents, sisters and grandmother at 80, Wood Street, Stockport. His brother and sister in law lived at 6, Napier Street, Hazel Grove, but whether Arthur himself had lived in the village is not known. The records show that he was born in Stockport and enlisted in the Welch Fusiliers in Stockport.

George Arthur Vernon is commemorated on the Memorial at Mikra, Greece, and also on the Memorial at Stockport Art Gallery.

~~~~~~

# Captain Stephen Wynn **Vickers** M.C. D.F.C.
## 200 Squadron   R.A.F.
## 19 February 1919
(Picture)

The Foundation Stone of Norbury Church was laid on 13 May 1833 and it is doubtful whether in the 86 intervening years there was a grander funeral than that given to Stephen Vickers on 22 February 1919. He is the most decorated man on the War Memorial, but his family never actually lived in Hazel Grove.

Born in Hunslet, Leeds, on 9 October 1895, he was the son of James and Elizabeth Vickers. James was a schoolmaster who came to Stockport to become the Headmaster of Great Moor School. The family lived at 408, Buxton Road, Great Moor, but worshipped regularly at Norbury Church. They are remembered as a rather 'aloof' family who did not mix with the other parishioners.

After being educated at his father's school, Great Moor, Stephen went to Stockport Grammar School.  He was one of the original members of one of the first Scout Groups in Stockport - 1st Davenport, which he joined in 1908. Eventually he became Assistant Scoutmaster with the 3rd Stockport Scouts (St. George's) and was a King's Scout.

It was his intention to go to Owen's College (Manchester University) in October 1914, but when war broke out on 4 August 1914,  he volunteered for a Commission in the Army and was gazetted as a 2nd Lieutenant on 17 September 1914, being posted to the 11th Battalion Cheshire Regiment on the 19th September. He was 18 years old. The Stockport Express of 13 May 1915 has a picture of Lieutenant Vickers together with his platoon of Signallers of the 11th Cheshires. He served with this and the 14th Battalion in France until April 1916 when he was severely wounded at Vimy Ridge whilst on observation duty.

His wounds were such that he was brought back to England, but he made a quick recovery and volunteered to join the Royal Flying Corps. They accepted him on 4 September 1916. By now he was 20 and his next of kin - his mother, was living at 22, Countess Street, Heaviley. Training in the 26th, 58th, 63rd and 11th Squadrons followed and he showed considerable aptitude as a Night Flying Bomber Pilot. On 25 July 1917 he went to France with a newly formed squadron of night bombers - 101 Squadron. On 2 October 1917 however, he received a knee injury which made it neccessary for him to be admitted to 7th General Hospital at St. Omer in France where he stayed until the 23rd of that month. The cause of the injury is not noted. It may have been a wound or it could have happened as a result of a very heavy landing.

On 27 October 1917, Stephen was posted back to 101 Squadron to continue his night bombing activities, which he did with such gusto that on the 14 April 1918 he was

140

awarded the Military Cross. The citation in the London Gazette of 22 June 1918 is as follows :-

" For conspicuous gallantry and devotion to duty. He has taken part in 53 night bombing raids on enemy aerodromes, billets and communications, flying at times in most unfavourable weather and in the face of intense rifle and machine gun fire. On two occasions he made three flights in one night, reaching his objective on each occasion and doing considerable damage with direct hits. He has set a splendid example of courage and determination to the rest of his squadron."

Events moved fast. He was promoted to Captain on 19 April, and by the time the citation for the MC had been published, Stephen had been honoured again. On 3 June 1918, the London Gazette announced the award to him of the Distinguished Flying Cross in the King's Birthday Honours List as by then he had completed 75 successful raids over enemy territory at night. It was then decided that he should be sent home for a well earned rest, but soon he was posted again , this time to 200 Squadron which was a training squadron based at Harpswell, about 10 miles north of Lincoln. It had been decided to use his skills in the training of new recruits.

Cruel fate then took a hand. Stephen Vickers contacted pneumonia, probably during the great influenza pandemic which swept the world in 1918, killing more people than were killed in the war. He died in the 4th Northern General Hospital at Lincoln on 19th February 1919.

Reports in both the local newspapers contained tributes to him together with comments as to the kind of person he was. He was described as having "an engaging personality" and being "loved and respected by all with whom he came into contact". His Sergeant Major wrote - "He was a perfect gentleman; kind and considerate; with a high ideal of the duties which he had to perform." Another eulogy said amongst many other things that he was 6ft. 2ins. tall with a cheery voice, and was deeply respected and admired by his fellow officers. It also pointed out that he had been put in charge of a company direct from school at the age of 19. Even taking into account the fact that only the nicest things are said about most people when they die, he was clearly an exceptional person.

The funeral on Saturday 22nd February was extremely impressive, as one would expect for a local war hero. Full military honours were given. The coffin was borne to the grave by eight of his brother officers, attended by three senior warrant officers and the route through the Churchyard was lined by members of St. George's Scout Troop where he had been a member for many years. A large number of mourners attended, including local dignitaries.

At the conclusion of the service, the coffin was carried to the grave, three volleys were fired and the 'Last Post' sounded. He was buried in grave AD13 and was 23 years old. The grave still exists. It is a family grave, not a CWGC stone, and is immediately next to the south wall of the new extension, at the side of the door. His name is also on the Memorials at Norbury Church, St. George's Church, Stockport Grammar School and Stockport Art Gallery.

# 17946 Lance Corporal Harold **Walters**
## 11th Bn Cheshire Regiment
## 3 July 1916
### (Picture)

It was on the third day of the Battle of the Somme that Harold Walters died, the second soldier from Hazel Grove to be a victim of it. Thirteen more were to follow before the Battle was over.

The first Thomas and Elizabeth Ann Walters of 35,Hatherlow Lane, knew of their son's death was when they received a letter from a friend of his, Corporal H. Adams, who had been wounded and was convalescing in Hospital at Marple. He wrote - "Harold was killed by a machine gun bullet on the morning of July 3rd. He had just come in after being over the top and was hit by a shot which hit him in the back and doubled him round. I thought he was dead, for I was going to see him when I was hit by shrapnel. I was a big pal of his, in fact we have been together since we enlisted in November 1914. I hope you will receive this letter and think of the best. He was a good lad and well liked and did his duty as well as any man wearing uniform,"

Receipt of this letter 'prostrated' Mrs. Walters and she had to take to her bed for a few days. It was whilst she was in this condition that the official notification of Harold's death was received.

There had been a massive artillery barrage which had lasted for several days before the Battalion attacked Thiepval, and it was thought that this would have destroyed everything in sight, but all it did was make the advance more difficult. The terrain became chaotic and the Germans were safe in deep shelters. When the barrage stopped, they came up and were able to easily pick off the British troops as they struggled across the devastated No Man's Land.

During the first three days of the Battle, the Battalion was met by a constant withering fire of machine guns until it had simply 'wasted away'. The Colonel and every Company Commander were killed and by the morning of the 4th July, no organised body of men existed. Twenty officers and 657 men went into the attack and by 4th July, only 6 officers and 50 men remained.

Harold was baptised at St. George's Church, Poynton on 25 November 1894 when his parents lived in Poynton, his father being a collier. The family later moved to Hazel Grove. Before the war, Harold had worked for Williams & Sons, Wholesale Grocers of Reddish, and had joined the Cheshire Regiment at the age of 19. He went to France in September 1915 and had managed to get one spell of Home Leave between then and his death in July 1916.

A regular attender at the Primitive Methodist Church, Harold was given a Memorial Service there on Sunday 6th August, during which the Minister, Rev. Abijah Heaton, referred to his energetic work in connection with the Church and Sunday School. Harold was so involved with the Church that he had sent his annual subscription from the front only a few weeks before his death. The choir sang the anthem 'What are these arrayed in white' and a new setting to the hymn 'Jerusalem my happy home'. At the end of the service, Mr. Fidler the organist, played 'The Dead March'.

Like many of the victims of those horrendous days, Harold's body was never found and he is therefore one of the 73,000 missing, commemorated on the Memorial at Thiepval, France, as well as being on the Primitive Methodist section of the Memorial at the Methodist Church. He was 21 years old. His death was not only a blow to his family and to his church, but it was also a great blow to the Holebrook family, for his mother, Elizabeth Ann, was the daughter of Allan Holebrook (Senior) and therefore the sister of Charles and Reginald  and the Aunt of Allan (Junior), all three of whom were to die before the war ended.

~~~~~~

# 2nd Lieutenant Stanley **Warburton**
## 12th Bn Lancashire Fusiliers
## 14 September 1916
(Picture)

Stanley Warburton was one of the two sons of Thomas and Martha Ellen Warburton whose address when the CWGC compiled their records in 1921 was 'Woodside', Poynton and it is not clear what his connection with Hazel Grove was. 'Woodside' was situated between Poynton Pool and Park Lane, Poynton and therefore some distance from Hazel Grove. Perhaps the family had lived in Hazel Grove during the war for Stanley's name is not on the Memorial at Poynton.

Stanley was in fact a brilliant student. He had attended Macclesfield Grammar School and then gone on to Manchester University where, in 1911 he received his B.A.. His Teaching Diploma was obtained in 1912, as was his Teaching Certificate and he went on to receive his M.A. in 1913. Whilst at Manchester University, he was a member of the O.T.C., secretary of the Lacrosse Club and a member of the fencing team.

Obtaining a post as Classics Master at Colston School, Stapleton near Bristol (a 'Bluecoat' School which still exists), an academic career was ahead, but the war intervened and in March 1915 he was commissioned into the 12th Battalion, Lancashire Fusiliers, being sent to the front in August of that same year. In Stanley's case however, the front was not in France or Belgium but in the Balkans, where the fighting was bitter and spasmodic.

He was posted to 'D' Coy., and was put in charge of the machine guns. By September 1916, the battalion was near a place called Macuovo and on the 14th was ordered to attack a hill named Piton de Mitrailleuses which was occupied by the Bulgarians. The hill was part of a huge razor-backed ridge and was immensely fortified. The positions were a series of fortified knolls, rising one behind the other, and protected by crossfire from a convenient spur. The enemy positions were almost immune to shell fire but a heavy bombardment of the Bulgar trenches took place and their positions were captured easily with a considerable number of Bulgars being killed or taken prisoner. During the day, the enemy made repeated counter attacks and the shellfire on the captured positions was extremely heavy, causing many casualties. At dusk, orders were received to evacuate the hill and the battalion withdrew to its original position. Losses were very heavy, with 200 being killed, wounded or missing, including 5 officers, one of whom was Stanley Warburton. The attack never had any chance of success, but was made to pin the Bulgarians down while the Serbs swung round the right flank.

Stanley Warburton has no known grave and is commemorated on the Memorial at Doiran, in Northern Greece, as well as on the Memorial at Macclesfield Grammar School. He was 26 years old.

~~~~~~

144

# 25268 Private Joseph **Welbourn**
## 15th Bn Cheshire Regiment
### 18 April 1917

Joseph Welbourn, the son of Thomas, a bricklayer's labourer and Sarah Ann Welbourn, is shown in the 1891 Census as living at 3, Smithy Street with his parents and family, and he is said to be 13 years old and a cotton operative.

The 15th Battalion, Cheshire Regiment was a 'Bantam' Regiment, in other words, its recruits were below 5ft. 4ins tall, but Joseph Welbourn may not have been. In order to provide some solidity, a few experienced soldiers were attached to the regiment. Joseph was certainly experienced, in fact, he had served in the Boer War and had 18 years Army service behind him. It is not clear when he left the Army, but it was several years before the start of the war, because he had been employed by a company named Edwards & Co of Manchester for some time before he re-enlisted on 1st February 1915 at 39 years of age. This does not quite tie in with the age given on the Census, but as only one person of that name died in the War, there is no doubt that he is the correct person. His wife and four children remained at 6, Newbridge Lane, Stockport as he went off for the second time to 'do his bit', but this time he did not return.

It was not only the British who suffered during the Battle of the Somme. The Germans also did, and as a result of their losses, on 24 February 1917 they started to withdraw to a previously constructed line of fortifications which became known as "The Hindenburg Line". Cautiously the British followed them, finding that the Germans had pursued a "Scorched Earth" policy and that little, if anything was left standing.

By April 1917 the withdrawal was complete, and the British now had to construct defences for themselves in front of, and overlooked by, the immense, previously planned and built German fortifications. Near Maissemmy, about 7 kms west of St. Quentin, the 15th Battalion Cheshire Regiment occupied an old German defence line. This was a less than wise move as the Germans knew exactly where it was and were able to deluge it at will with shellfire. On 18 April 1917 they did just this, killing Joseph and a number of his colleagues.

Joseph Welbourn is buried nearby at Roisel Community Cemetery Extension, France, in Plot III, Row K, Grave 10. He was 41 years old. His name is also on the Memorial at Stockport Art Gallery.

~~~~~

# 42024 Private Herbert **Williamson**
## Depot Battalion Loyal North Lancashire Regiment
## 15 December 1918

Herbert Williamson was baptised at Norbury Church on 25 May 1880, the son of Samuel Williamson, a joiner, and his wife Clara. Their address was simply given as 'Norbury'. The 1891 Census, however, gives their address as 2, Brook Street and Herbert was 11 years old. The Norbury School Log Book shows that on 17 March 1893 he left school to take up full time work - he was 13 years old. He became a painter, and on 17 June 1911, whilst living at 308, London Road, he married Lydia Willetts of Heaton Moor. When he died, Herbert's address was 20, Hazel Street. At 22, Hazel Street in 1918, lived the wife of Charles Oldham, who died less than a fortnight after him. Herbert's sister married George Ridgway, the brother of Jack Ridgway, who was killed on 29 September 1918.

Herbert was severely wounded and whilst in hospital in France, had one of his legs amputated. This, together with his other wounds, made him very depressed and recovery was taking a long time. He spent some time in Stepping Hill Hospital but as recovery was still a long way off, he was moved to Victoria Hospital, Stretford.

In an effort to assist, he was given a day's leave, but at tea time on the evening of Sunday 15th December 1918 he became very restless, got up from the table and went out into the back yard. His brother in law (Mr. Brunt) was concerned about him and, on hearing a strange noise and thinking him to be ill, went out to see what was the matter. There, he found Herbert lying on the ground with his throat cut. A razor was at his side and he was dead.

The Coroner, Mr. A.E.Fearns, held an inquest in Hazel Grove on the afternoon of Tuesday 17th December and a verdict of 'Suicide whilst of unsound mind' was returned. Sometimes, a person who committed suicide was denied burial in consecrated ground, but happily this was not the case with Herbert. Even so, it created a considerable furore in the village, which must have added to the distress of Lydia and their two young children, Irene Jane (born 15 August 1912) and Samuel (born 3 January 1914).

Clearly, Herbert must have been in a fighting battalion and not the Depot Battalion when he was wounded, but as he had been in hospital for some time, the decision must have been made to transfer him into the Depot Battalion.

Herbert was buried in grave 189 in Norbury Churchyard on 19th December 1918, at the age of 38. His wife Lydia was buried in the same grave after her death on 13th May 1958. The grave is not a CWGC gravestone, presumably because Lydia is buried there. It still exists - a pink marble cross, near the Rose Garden, and Herbert's name is on the Memorial in the church.

# 27040 Corporal Norman **Wilson**
## 9th Bn Loyal North Lancashire Regiment
## 10 April 1918

Another casualty of the German Spring Offensive of 1918 was Norman Wilson, the son of Henry Hough Wilson and his wife Sarah, of 'Jessiefield', Marple Road, Offerton. Offerton was part of Hazel Grove at the time and Jessiefield was the strip of land between Marple Road and Marple Old Road, near the 'Seventeen Windows'. Presumably the house was in that area.

Norman was born in Offerton and enlisted in the Manchester Regiment in Manchester but was transferred into the Loyal North Lancashire Regiment. The 9th Battalion was one of the battalions involved in attempting to stem the German advance right from the day it started on 21st March 1918 and took very heavy casualties throughout the period. During March, they had 23 killed, 124 wounded and 216 missing.

At the end of March they were withdrawn and sent to the Ploegsteert Sector in Belgium, but at 11am on 9th April, news was received that the Germans had attacked south of Armentieres as far as Givenchy. The attack succeeded in taking considerable portions of the British Line.

The Battalion was therefore ordered to move south to help out and by 4pm were in touch with the enemy at Steenweerk. At 3am on the 10th, the Battalion counter attacked, but the first attack failed to dislodge the enemy, who had numerous machine guns sited around the village of Croix du Bac. A further attack was therefore ordered at 4.30am. This succeeded, and the Battalion went straight through the village and established itself on the banks of the River Lys.

Unfortunately, the units on the Battalion's left were not as successful, with the result that the Loyal North Lancs. were enfiladed by machine gun fire, thus suffering heavy casualties. At about 7am they were forced to withdraw from the riverbank. At 9am however, they were ordered to try to force the Germans across the river again, but the enemy had received strong reinforcements and between 10.30am and 3.30pm they succeeded in getting round the British flanks, forcing the Battalion to withdraw once more.

Some time during the day, Norman Wilson was killed and his body was never found. His name is therefore on the Memorial to the Missing at Ploegsteert, Belgium. He was 37 years of age.

# 53991 Private George **Wood**
## 4th Bn Cheshire Regiment
## 14 October 1918

Within five days of William and Anne Wood of 11, Neville Street, being informed of the death in action of their second son Henry, they were informed that their third son, 18 year old George, had been wounded. Less than a month later, the war ended. Then they were told that George was missing. Some time later it was decided that he should be declared 'killed in action'

George was born in Hazel Grove and enlisted in the Cheshire Regiment in Chester. The 4th Battalion had spent most of the war in Palestine, but was transferred to France in July 1918, no doubt due to the German offensive which had pushed the British back many miles and was beginning to threaten Paris. In view of George's age, it is not clear whether he volunteered earlier when under age or joined the Battalion round about the time it went to France.

By October 1918 the pendulum had swung the way of the Allies and the Germans were being pushed back along most of the Western Front. It was at last becoming increasingly clear that the war would soon be over. The fighting still had to go on however, and on 11th October, the 4th took up a position in an open trench and old German pill boxes close to Gheluve (near Courtrai). On the night of 13 October they began their assault, during which they captured several guns and 110 Germans. The Battalion's losses were 166 killed, wounded and missing, one of whom was George Wood.

At first it was not known what had happened to him and he was posted 'missing'. The family put an advertisement in the Stockport Express of 9th January 1919, asking whether any returned Prisoner of War had any information about him and if they did, to contact his father. No good news came and he was later declared 'killed in action'. In less than a month, Mr. and Mrs. Wood had lost two of their sons.

George's body was never found. His name is on the Memorial Wall at Tyne Cot Cemetery, Near Ypres, Belgium and also on the Primitive Methodist section of the Memorial at the Methodist Church.

~~~~~

# 26354 Private Henry **Wood**
## 1st Bn Kings Shropshire Light Infantry
## 19 September 1918
(Picture)

William and Anne Wood had three sons serving in the forces. The eldest had been discharged, wounded and, five days after receiving the news on 9th October 1918 that their middle son Henry had been killed three weeks before, they received news that their youngest son George had been wounded. Later they were to find that George too, had died, leaving them with only one son.

Henry Wood had originally enlisted in the Cheshire Regiment at Stockport, but was later transferred into the KSLI. He first went to France in January 1916, but with which regiment is not known. During his 2 years 8 months at the front, he was wounded once and had also suffered from Trench Foot. He was killed, like his brother, whilst the Allies were beginning to force the Germans back to their eventual defeat.

The ground originally lost in the period from March to August 1918 was slowly being regained and at 5.20am on the morning of September 18th 1918, the 1st Battalion KSLI was on the left of an attack on a German strongpoint near Fresnoy, France. There was heavy rainfall during the night and as dawn broke, the morning mist obscured all landmarks, making the attack very difficult, with the result that the entire Brigade became hopelessly mixed up. Although progress was made, the ultimate objective was not reached.

At 1.30am on the 19th, orders were received to renew the attack on Fresnoy le Petit at 5.30am. which was duly done, B Coy. managing to reach the village, although it lost all its officers in the process. They then became isolated in the village and had to spend the rest of the day fighting off counter attacks. During the day, there were 176 casualties including Henry Wood.

Henry, who was 21 years old, was buried at Chapelle British Cemetery, in Plot III, Row D, Grave 6 and his name is also on Primitive Methodist section of the Memorial at the Methodist Church.

~~~~~

# 15626 Sergeant James **Worthington**
## 51st Coy.  Machine Gun Corps
## 12 October 1917

James Worthington lived with his father, also James, at 5, Pownall Street. James (senior) was a skin dealer. Pownall Street was the street which now leads to the Kwik Save Supermarket.

Like many others, James's death was not reported in the local newspapers, but unlike most of them, it has been impossible to find out much about him. The records show however, that he was born in Stockport but went to Winchester to enlist in the Kings Royal Rifle Corps. In early 1916 however, he transferred into the newly formed Machine Gun Corps, probably because he was a machine gunner in the KRRC. Although he was only 20 years old, he had been promoted to Sergeant.

As the MGC was spread throughout the various Divisions of the Army, it is not possible to say precisely where James was when he died. His unit of the MGC was attached to 51 Brigade and took part in the 3rd Battle of Ypres which commenced in appalling weather on 31 July 1917. The dreadful weather continued throughout the following three months the battle lasted, and by October the ground was a total morass. The Division was not far from the ruins of the village of Poelcappelle which, literally translated, means ' the Church in the swamp'. Before the land was drained and farmed, this is precisely what it was and now, because three years constant heavy artillery fire had totally destroyed every little bit of the drainage, it had returned to that state with a vengeance. The front was just a string of mud filled shell-holes and the ground was a waste of liquid mud cratered with shell-holes, ruined farms converted into strongpoints and concrete pill-boxes.

Zero hour for the British attack on 12 October was 5.25am. There had been heavy rain the day before and during the night, as the troops assembled, there began a downpour of cold rain which lasted for hours. The Brigade's objective was to push the enemy's front line back 600 yards in two successive bounds. Under a steady downpour the British artillery barrage began and the infantry advance started at the same time. The German counter barrage was not as heavy as usual and as a result, British casualties were lighter than expected. By 8.30am their objectives had been achieved and reinforcements were rushed up to help with the defence of these, although fighting continued nearby all day. Whilst the battle for Paschendaele continued for another month two miles to the East, it was decided that further attacks could not take place at Poelcappelle as the ground was absolutely impassable.

James's body was never found and his name is on the Memorial Wall at Tyne Cot Cemetery, near Ypres, and he is also commemorated on the Congregational Church Memorial at the United Reformed Church.

~~~~~~

# 41962 Private Edwin **Young**
## 2nd Bn South Wales Borderers
## 14 October 1918

Although he was born in Manchester, Edwin Young was living in Hazel Grove when he went to Stockport to enlist in the South Wales Borderers. Unfortunately, the CWGC records contain no details of his next of kin, but the 1918 Electoral Roll shows Edwin and Maria Louise Young living at 'Denbigh Villa', Chester Road. They were still there in the 1919 Roll, so it is distinctly possible that they were Edwin's parents.

Edwin died of wounds, and there are no details of the date he received his wounds, so we cannot be certain as to the circumstances under which they were received. For the two weeks prior to his death, his Battalion were in and out of the front line outside Ypres, being on the receiving end of several large barrages. On 12th October, they were in the vicinity of Dadizele, to the north of Menin where, despite hostile shelling, including gas shells, they were employed cutting gaps in the wire and patrolling No Man's Land.

On 13th October, they were relieved by 2 Bn Royal Fusiliers at 8pm and withdrew to the jumping off trenches. The War Diary makes no mention of any specific activities on the 14th, except to note that one 'Other Rank' was killed and nine wounded. Edwin has no known grave, despite the records stating that he died of wounds. This suggests that he died near the front and that he was not evacuated to hospital. It is very possible therefore that he was one of the casualties on the14th October.

Edwin Young is commemorated on the Memorial Wall at Tyne Cot Cemetery, near Ypres, Belgium, along with nine other men from Hazel Grove.

~~~~

# SOURCES OF PHOTOGRAPHS

## *Cheshire Year Books*

### *1917*

| | |
|---|---|
| Walter Adshead | p147 |
| Frank Clough | p185 |
| Samuel Condliffe | p213 |
| Arthur Daniels | p147 |
| Joseph Hallworth (S. Lancs.Regt.) | p85 |
| Frank Jackson | p147 |
| John Marsland | p147 |
| Frederick Rowbotham | p147 |
| Frederick Taylor | p147 |
| Harold Walters | p122 |
| Stanley Warburton | p185 |

### *1918*

| | |
|---|---|
| Joseph Bannister | p41 |
| Henry Bowers | p127 |
| George Brown | p141 |
| Ernest Dean | p141 |
| Charles Holebrook | p141 |
| John Martin | p141 |
| Frank Middlebrooke | p141 |

### *1919*

| | |
|---|---|
| Edward Axon | p166 |
| Frederick Clarke | p128 |
| Stanley Clough | p128 |
| Frank Hallam | p128 |
| Joseph Hallworth (Chesh. Regt.) | p115 |
| William Hallworth | p115 |
| Clifford Holt | p166 |
| Arnold Jones | p115 |
| Louis Jones | p115 |
| John Ridgway | p115 |
| George Stubbs | p128 |
| George Tallent | p128 |
| Winson Tallent | p128 |
| Henry Wood | p115 |

## *Stockport Advertiser*

| | |
|---|---|
| Gerald Griffiths | 3 January 1919 |
| Gilbert Stanton | 11 June 1915 |
| Stephen Vickers | 28 February 1919 |

## *Stockport Express*

| | |
|---|---|
| Samuel Adshead | 21 June 1917 |
| Frank Daniels | 23 January 1919 |
| Robert Gee | 6 June 1918 |
| Arthur Henshall | 10 October 1918 |
| Herbert Hooley | 20 September 1917 |
| James Swindells | 3 January 1918 |
| Harold Taylor | 15 November 1917 |
| Joseph Welbourn | 17 May 1917 |
| George Wood | 9 January 1919 |

Note - Only Microfilm copies of The Stockport Express are held at Stockport Heritage Library. Locally held copies of the originals no longer exist (and are not held by the newspaper), so it has not been possible to include photographs of the above in this book.

## *Miscellaneous*

| | |
|---|---|
| Geoffrey Bagshawe | Harrow Memorials of The Great War |
| Frederick Bann | Mr. K. Daniels |
| John Clarke | Mrs. E. Warren |
| Allan Holebrook | Mrs. M. Cook |
| Reginald Holebrook | Mrs. M. Cook |
| Daniel Kilday | Mr. B. Kilday |
| Harold Skeen | Mr. J. Skeen |
| Front and back covers | The Manchester Guardian History of the War |
| Opening Ceremony of Hazel Grove War Memorial (11 November 1923) | Stockport Library Collection |

~~~~~

# SOURCES USED IN THIS BOOK

**Manuscripts etc.**

Hazel Grove and Bramhall UDC Minutes.
Mirrlees, Bickerton & Day Ltd. - Apprentice Books.
Norbury School Log Books.
St. George's Church, Poynton.  Baptism Register.
St. Thomas' Church, Norbury.  Baptism, Marriage and Burial Registers.
War Diaries :  Cheshire Regiment.
      Duke of Wellington's Regiment.
      King's Own Royal Regiment of Lancaster.
      Monmouthshire Regiment.
      Northumberland Fusiliers.
      Notts & Derby Regiment.
      Seaforth Highlanders.
      South Wales Borderers.
      Welch Regiment

**Newspapers**

Stockport Advertiser
Stockport Express
Cheshire Year Books, 1915-1920.
London Gazette

**Directories etc**

1907 Street Directory of Hazel Grove.
1910 Street Directory of Hazel Grove.
Registers of The General Register Office.
Hazel Grove and Bramhall UDC - 1918 Electoral Roll.
Hazel Grove and Bramhall UDC - 1919 Electoral Roll.

**Census**

1891 Census of Hazel Grove.

## Books

An Account of the 22nd Battalion (Manchester Regiment) in France, Belgium, Italy and Egypt. (1922)

Sidney **Allinson** : The Bantams. (1981)

C T **Atkinson** : The History of The Royal Dragoons, 1661- 1934. (1934)

A Hilliard **Atteridge** : The History of the 17th (Northern) Division. (1929)

The Bond of Sacrifice: A record of all the British Officers who fell in The Great War. Vol. II (1915)

Robert **Bonner** : The 12th Battalion. Manchester Regiment 1914-1918. (1994)

A **Crookenden** : The History of The Cheshire Regiment in The Great War. (1925)

**CWGC** : The 58th Division in France & Flanders. (undated)

**CWGC** : Records of the Commonwealth War Graves Commission. (1921)

John **Giles** : Flanders Then and Now. (1987)

Forster **Groom** : Regimental Records of The Royal Welch Fusiliers. (undated)

Harrow Memorials of The Great War. (1918)

**Hazel Grove Local History Group** : Hazel Grove-T'other end o' village (1985)

The History of the 16th - 19th Battalions : Manchester Regiment. (1922)

The History of The North Staffordshire Regiment. 1914-1923. (1933)

**HMSO** : Soldiers Died in The Great War. (1921)

Charles **Hocking** : Dictionary of Disasters at Sea during the age of Steam. Vol. I (1969)

L **Hughes** & J **Dixon** : 'Surrender Be Damned'. 1st Monmouthshire Regimental History. (1995)

David **Kelsall** : Stockport Lads Together. (1989)

J C **Latter** : The History of The Lancashire Fusiliers. (1949)

Manchester Guardian History of The War. Vol V (1916), Vol IX (1920)

The Manchester University Register of Graduates. (1933)

Sir Thomas O. **Marden** : The History of The Welsh Regiment : Part II. (1932)

Maj.Gen. T O **Marden** : A Short History of the 6th Division. 1914-1918. (1920)

Chris **McCarthy** : The Somme. The Day by Day Account. (1993)

N **Mcleod** : The War History of the 6th Bn Queens Own Cameron Highlanders.(1934)

G W L **Nicholson** : The Canadian Expeditionary Force 1914-1918. (1962)

C **Platt** : 150 years of Education-Norbury C of E Primary School. (1985)

Roll of Honour. The London and North Western Railway Company. (undated)

A Short History of The 22nd or Cheshire Regiment. (1936)

Michael **Steadman** : Manchester Pals. (1994)

D H **Trowsdale** : The History of Hazel Grove. (1976)

Norman H **Turner** : The Norbury Parish Story. (1984)

H **Whaley-Kelly** : 'Ich Dien'. The Prince of Wales Volunteers (South Lancashire) (1935)

W de B **Wood** : The History of The King's Shropshire Light Infantry in The Great War. 1914-1918. (1925)

H C **Wylly** : The Loyal North Lancashire Regiment. Vol II. 1914-1918. (1933)

Everard **Wyrrall** :The 'Diehards in The Great War'. The Regimental History of The Middlesex Regiment. (1920)

Everard **Wyrrall** : The History of The King's Regiment (Liverpool). Vol III. (1935)